To Bettina
With love,
Ruth and Rachel
Feb. 2, 1999

T W I N S

Photographs by David Fields

Essays by Ruth and Rachel Sandweiss

T W I N S

Running Press
Philadelphia • London

9 8 7 6 5 4 3 2 1
Digit on the right indicates the number of this printing.

Library of Congress
Cataloging-in-Publication Number 98-65548
ISBN 0-7624-0404-3

This book is set in Perpetua and Frutiger.
Printed in China.

This book may be ordered by mail from the publisher.
Please include $2.50 for postage and handling.
But try your bookstore first!

Running Press Book Publishers
125 South Twenty-second Street
Philadelphia, Pennsylvania 19103-4399

Dedications
Acknowledgments

To twins, our family, and God, who created all this mystery, marvel, and love.

Our deepest thanks to our family—our parents, Samuel and Sharon, who have been a source of constant love and ever-willing support; Beth and Judy, close confidantes whose sisterly love has kept us smiling, grounded, and balanced, and who have encouraged us with the constant reminder, "You can do it!"; Grandma Freda, whose wisdom and vision have guided us since day one; and all other family members, including Chessie, Woolly Bear, and Bo Bear.

We wish to thank our many wonderful friends and co-workers for their encouragement and appreciation of our twin relationship. We are also very grateful to the special people who helped transform this project from a dream to a reality—Patty Smith, Tara McFadden, David Fields, and others at Running Press Book Publishers. A special thanks to our agent, Dick Croy, who was there with expertise and caring at a very crucial moment, transcriptionist Sarah Hunt, and twin support and resource groups.

Finally, a heartfelt thanks to the extraordinary people in this book.

—*RDS and RDS*

•   •   •

For my family

I wish to thank Ken Newbaker for his support during this project; Chuck Kelton and his staff for making a beautiful collection of prints for the book; and my grandmother, Nettie Ribak, who is the best assistant in all of Florida. Above all, though, my greatest thanks go to the wonderful twins who allowed me to take their portraits.

—*DF*

Contents

Jill (left) and Jacqueline Hennessy
photographed in New York City.

Preface

What's it like to be a twin? In our thirty-one years together as identical twins, this single most commonly asked question is also the hardest to answer. The fact is, we don't know what it's like *not* to be a twin. We just feel blessed to have each other—a best friend and confidante with whom we can share everything.

Ever since we were little, we dreamed of working on a project together. And what project could be closer to our hearts than one focusing on the deep, unspoken bond between twins?

When we began to create this book with photographer David Fields, we knew that every twin relationship would be different. But after talking with many sets of twins, we began to see patterns. This helped us better understand our relationship and how our unique bond affects other relationships.

We found that above all else most twins appreciate their close bond. It is striking to see the warmth and affection between ninety-four-year-old twins Marion Bartholomew and Minerva Lipp, who have lived together for the past twenty-two years since being widowed. And Abigail and Brittany Hensel, seven-year-old conjoined twins, could teach the world wonders about cooperation and camaraderie.

To many twins, their bond is a source of great inner strength. Joseph and Boris Fisch survived the atrocities of the Holocaust together because of their unwavering devotion and support.

The twin bond sometimes contributes to an innate, collaborative, shared ambition with each twin helping the other to reach a greater level of success. Doctors Robert and Ralph Mendez helped each other reach a greater level of success working together in kidney transplantation.

Many twins struggle to find a balance between their closeness and their individuality. Twenty-one-year-old Kurt and Kyle Froman, dancers for the New York City Ballet, experienced deeper friendship only after they better developed their own identities—by moving into separate apartments.

At the same time, attempts to distinguish between twins may unintentionally create competition and resentment. College students MyLe and MyAn Zagorsky learned how to overcome competition by supporting each other toward different goals.

Being a twin also affects other relationships. Jill and Jacqueline Hennessy feel that being twins has contributed to their ability to develop intimacy in other relationships. On the other hand, these relationships may be threatening to the twin relationship. Jamillah Ali and Rasheda Ali-Walsh, as well as Tia and Tamera Mowry, admit that it can be lonely when one of them spends more time with her spouse or boyfriend.

Jealousies may also arise in friends, boyfriends, and siblings who find it difficult to compete with the twin alliance.

Parents of twins face special choices—whether to separate twins into different classrooms, how to provide equal attention to all siblings in the family, and how to raise twins as individuals while appreciating their bond, as Jane Seymour and James Keach discuss. Parents explore these and other issues at national and local chapters of Mothers of Twins Clubs.

• • •

People throughout history have been fascinated by twin births, and this interest has been intensified by events such as the McCaughey family's milestone of 1997, the first successful birth of septuplets. We would have liked to include stories of multiple births of three or more children—often referred to as *supertwins*—in this book and to address important issues specific to this rapidly growing population. However, the social, ethical, health, and financial concerns of this population could not be adequately covered in a few short essays, and they deserve to be the focus of their own book. For information about multiple birth support groups, readers can contact supertwins support networks, the Triplet Connection and Mothers of Supertwins (MOST).

While identical twin rates are relatively constant and universal, fraternal twin rates vary among countries and ethnic groups and have increased significantly in the last ten years. This rise in fraternal twin births is due to the increased use of fertility drugs and the growing number of women delaying childbirth as well as to improved prenatal care and advances in medical technology.

Twins remain an intriguing mystery—on a biological, psychological, and, some feel, spiritual level. Scientists have found them fascinating subjects for the study of human behavior and personality development, offering a special opportunity to investigate nature (genes) versus nurture (environment). Identical twins Jim Lewis and Jim Springer, for example, were separated at birth and reunited as adults—only to learn that they share extraordinary similarities in their lives, personalities, and behaviors. Other identical twins who were raised together, like Brady and Brian Ralston, have completely different personalities, interests, and sexual orientations.

Psychologists and theologians may look to twins for deeper understanding of human consciousness and communication. Do twins share telepathy or a "sixth" sense? Claudia Jefferson Beckman and Colleen Jefferson Hisdahl, for instance, report feeling their twin's pain even when they are separated by a great distance.

Twins may help us learn more about the way we form our own special identities. Most twins with whom we've spoken agree that having the same genes will never make two people *exactly* the same.

We deeply treasure our twin bond and want to celebrate the twin experience through these photographs and essays.

We offer this book to twins and non-twins alike, with the hope that the stories touch your heart as they have ours, eradicate common misconceptions, illuminate joys and challenges distinct to twins, and give you a deeper understanding of one of the most precious and rewarding human bonds. Most important, we hope this book sheds light on human relationships in a way that brings us all closer together.

John LaChappa
Joseph LaChappa

John and Joseph LaChappa, nine-month-old identical twins, were born into the Kumeyaay tribe on the Barona Indian Reservation in San Diego, California.

The birth of twins in the Kumeyaay tribe has always been considered a blessing, a sign of good luck and prosperity often associated with supernatural forces. *Haawaak*, the Kumeyaay word for twins, conjures up a powerful mythical image. According to legend, the gods who created the tribe—*tu·čaypa·* and *Yokomatis*—were twins.

John and Joseph's father, Eagle, their mother, Shannon, their grandmother Linda and grandfather Clifford Sr., Chief of the Barona Indian Reservation, all consider it an honor to have twins in the family. For them, the symbolic link to Kumeyaay history is important for the preservation of their heritage.

"I really want John and Joseph to have an American Indian background," Eagle emphasizes, "because the Indian heritage is dying, and so many Indians are disappearing. We're Kumeyaay Indians, the farthest Cheyenne tribe to come West."

John and Joseph, like their four-year-old sister, Cherish, and six-year-old brother, Cai, will learn to read from an Indian language book and participate in an Indian dance group when they get older. On Labor Day the entire family attends the annual powwow held in Barona, where Shannon and Eagle first met as teenagers.

"So," Clifford Sr. muses, "culture is kept. But it's hard—we've only got about four elders left in the tribe. All the rest of them have died off. Respect is extremely important—you look to the elders for guidance. Times are also different now because thinking and values have changed."

He looks toward his twin grandsons—two developing strengths of the tribe—and is filled with hope. To the entire LaChappa family, John and Joseph represent the good luck and prosperity of the Kumeyaay twin tradition.

John (left) and Joseph La Chappa live on the Barona Indian Reservation, San Diego, California.

John Reiff
William Reiff

The stillness of May is interrupted by the sound of pigs eating from their troughs and cows settling in the barn. Two slim figures make their way in from one hundred and fifty acres of corn, oats, barley, and hay. Their slender frames move at the same even pace, and their conversation sounds almost like one person talking to himself.

It's difficult to tell just how old these Pennsylvania farmers are, but their chiseled, sun-weathered faces give some clue. "We are each thirty-four," says Bill, a mischievous glimmer in his eyes. Actually twice that age, John and Bill live on the family farm where they were born and raised. Their farmhouse is nestled on a lane that bears the family name. The Reiffs remember helping their father in the same fields, but the horse-drawn plow was long ago replaced by a large tractor.

The land is their home and livelihood, binding the brothers together with a strong work ethic and devotion to one another. "If I couldn't be with my brother and help him on the farm, I wouldn't be satisfied or happy," John explains with simple honesty. "You always know that you have somebody to work with or back you up. That's the whole thing of being twins."

John shares a story that describes the intangible connection between them. "In 1955, I caught my foot in a tractor pulley. Bill was down in the lower field on the opposite side of the house plowing with another tractor. He was about four blocks away and couldn't see or hear my tractor running. The tractor pulley tore my ankle socket completely out of my leg. I called for my father, who came down and helped me off the tractor, then sent a worker down to the field to let Billy know about me being hurt. Before he got even halfway down the back lane, Billy was halfway up."

"I knew right away that something had

John (left) and Bill Reiff stand by each
other on the family farm, Phoenixville, Pennsylvania.

13

happened to John," Bill interrupts, "but I didn't know what. I had the feeling that he got hurt."

"And it's only through the help of God and the doctor that I have my foot," John finishes. "Whenever Bill wasn't working on the farm, he'd come down to the hospital to spend the day or night with me."

Bill's support brought them closer together than ever.

"When the time came for us to get married location across the U.S. where the annual convention is held." John adds, "We enjoy being around other twins very much."

"The best thing about being a twin is the deep friendship and the closeness. I received my Army greetings in 1951 and was sent to Korea for thirteen months," John says. "Bill was exempted from serving because of the farm—there was enough ground there for one person to take care of. I was so worried about leaving Bill, I cried all the way down to my departure."

"It was dreadful," remembers Bill. "We kept in touch with each other, and when he would go up to the front lines he would send me letters telling me he was up there because I never knew what might happen to him."

"Bill even bought me an 8-mm movie camera, so I'd send movies home and he could see what I was doing firsthand."

But looking back, they agree that their fear during those months ultimately gave way to personal growth. "Maybe it was a good thing to be by ourselves to build confidence in ourselves, but we didn't know it," says Bill. "We had never been separated before. Maybe we were too close."

"If I couldn't be with my brother and help him on the farm, I wouldn't be satisfied or happy. That's the whole thing of being twins."

and to help on the farm," John says, "the woman I was dating wanted me just to herself. She told me, 'I didn't realize you were that close.' I don't know if she thought that we would separate or what."

"I wouldn't marry any woman if she wouldn't let me be with my brother when I wanted to. I just wouldn't have it," echoes Bill.

John and Bill strongly identify with their twinship. They attended their first International Twin Association (ITA) Convention in 1956 and have returned every year.

"We haven't missed one yet," Bill grins, proud of their forty-two years of attendance. "Each year we have to prepare and mix enough feed for the cows while we're gone. Then we travel to a new

They were reunited and haven't been apart since—and they don't intend to be, even in the event of marriage.

John and Bill seek twin female companions who understand their relationship. "We dated a set of twins in the past, but weren't ready to settle down," John explains. "We've been searching for a set of twins to marry for the last several years." The brothers seem to be enjoying their quest.

Meanwhile, John and Bill will continue to honor the family legacy as an undivided team, tending their land and animals with identical loving care. As John says, "We came into this world together and we hope to leave together."

MyAn Zagorsky
MyLe Zagorsky

"**I**n a way, our family started its own culture," says nineteen-year-old MyAn Zagorsky of her upbringing by her Polish father and Vietnamese mother. "I think we've gotten the best of both worlds. In Asian cultures, the oldest child carries the maternal name. In our case, MyLe was born first. 'My' means 'graceful' in Vietnamese, and 'Le' is our mom's maiden name. My name, MyAn, means 'graceful peace.' And our younger sister's name, MyLing, means 'graceful spirit.'"

"We've experienced and contributed to both the Vietnamese and Polish cultures," says her identical twin sister, MyLe. "We represented Vietnam in the Lorain International Festival pageant and were debutantes at the Polish ball."

"At the Lorain International Festival," adds MyAn, "we dressed as the Trung sisters—Trung Trac and Trung Nhi—twin sisters in Vietnamese history who came to symbolize heroism and independence after they led a successful military uprising against Chinese invaders in A.D. 40. We also celebrate the Vietnamese New Year, Tet, and have some traditional Asian values. Asian culture is very family-oriented. For example, when you own a business, the whole family is involved."

Their mother, TuLe Thi Zagorsky, owns two beauty salons, and her daughters have worked at each. They also have earned beautician's licenses.

"Our mom is Buddhist," says MyLe, "and sometimes we go with her to temple. But we were baptized and also practice Catholicism with our father."

And, like their father, James Paul Zagorsky, they observe several Polish traditions. "When we participated in the Polish Debutante Ball," MyLe continues, "we were presented to the Polish community and danced the polka."

The Zagorskys also share their father's interest in engineering. Both are currently working at a cooperative sponsored by Honda of America Manufacturing and Ohio State

MyLe (left) and MyAn Zagorsky visit Lake Erie near their home in Cleveland, Ohio.

University. "Later, in graduate school, we might study biomedicine or genetics," says MyLe.

The Zagorsky sisters are spirited college sophomores and are suite mates with six other women. They share a car, a part-time job, the same taste in clothes and men—and they love to double date.

"We even exercise together and put ourselves on the same diets together," laughs MyLe.

"We're a lot closer than the average twins," MyAn admits. "A lot of twins

"Since I ran for class president," recalls MyLe, "MyAn ran for homecoming queen. I helped her. And she won."

"We're best friends even though we fight a lot," confides MyAn. "A lot of people don't see that part—that there are struggles. It can be frustrating. Sometimes it's not for the best that twins are always together. People think it's all cake. 'Oh, you're twins. You're so lucky.' I do feel that we're really lucky, but sometimes I just need some space."

"Our psychology teacher said that she sees an interpersonal dependency. She claims that

They share a car, a part-time job, the same taste in clothes and men—and they love to double date.

I know went off in different directions during and after high school."

"But for us it was the opposite," muses MyLe. "We were separated all through elementary and junior high school. And then, in high school, we were in the same classes."

"The only thing we hate," MyAn notes, "is when people compare us competitively. 'Well, genetically you have the same potential, because you're twins. So how come she got an A and you got a C?'"

While many twins resent the pressure to be either exactly the same or completely different, the Zagorskys have discovered how to use the pressure to their combined advantage. When they encounter a goal that can be achieved by only one of them, it becomes a mutual challenge— they agree on who will attempt the goal and who will support the other's efforts.

"We share our individual successes," MyAn explains. For example, when elections came up for senior class president, we both said, 'Oh, I'd like to do that.' But if we both ran, we'd be splitting our votes, and chances were neither of us would win. So we decided that MyLe would run, and I was her campaign manager. It felt like I was running. And she ended up winning."

everything's a joint decision," explains MyLe. "We agree on most things, but it's still my own opinion. It's not because we're trying to mold ourselves after each other."

"The professor did have a little bit of a point," concedes MyAn. "A lot of people say, 'Split up, go your separate ways, blah, blah, blah.' But we've come to the conclusion that we're more successful when we work together."

Kurt Froman
Kyle Froman

"Ballet is pretty much our lives. I love ballet for the powerful art form that it is," Kurt Froman says, his voice and gestures displaying energy and passion. "It's incredible when good choreography and music come together."

Kurt sits next to his identical twin, Kyle, outside Lincoln Center, where the twenty-one-year-old brothers spend most of their time performing in the highly respected New York City Ballet with ninety talented ballet dancers.

"City Ballet is one of the best companies in the world . . . definitely in the United States," explains Kyle. "So, that was our goal—to join New York City Ballet."

"But I never thought I was good enough," admits Kurt.

"We could have gotten into New York City Ballet individually by our own talents," maintains Kyle. "As twins, it took some time to realize that and build confidence in our own dancing abilities. At the same time, although I hate using my being a twin as any kind of gimmick, I knew that the ballet company couldn't resist. New York City Ballet likes that sense of family. Plus, they like the look."

"Our musicality is almost exactly the same without our even consciously thinking, 'Oh, I'm going to dance like you,'" interjects Kurt. "Twins are kind of bonded subconsciously. When you look at tapes of us, we might be on different sides of the stage, but if you unfocus your eyes, it's like two people moving exactly the same."

"Even if nobody else is together," Kyle laughs, "we're together—right or wrong! I hardly ever notice that we dance alike. I just know that that's what people tell us. I've seen another set of twins, Amy and Laurel Foster, perform in Miami City Ballet. Watching them was great. I thought, 'Wow, that is cool.'"

Despite their likeness on the dance floor, Kyle

Kyle (left) and Kurt Froman dance in the New York City Ballet rehearsal studios.

and Kurt prefer to emphasize their distinctions rather than their similarities.

"One thing that I can't stand is when people say, 'Oh, the twins. Are you Kyle? No, Kurt. Oh, whatever, same thing,'" Kyle explains.

"I like hearing how people tell us apart—when people say, 'Okay, Kyle has a longer face, or Kurt has two different-colored eyes.' One is green, and one is more brown," Kurt points out with a smile. "I like when people make an effort to recognize 'these are your traits and these are his.' Especially since we're doing the same thing every day and working so hard to build a professional reputation for ourselves individually. Our personalities are very different. That's how most people tell us apart. Kyle's more internal and quiet. I'm more verbal, more open."

"We want people to notice our own style—to see subtleties and shadings in our dancing. We really are different," asserts Kyle. "As a dancer, you're

"We're so much closer now that we're living apart. We started talking more instead of holding back," states Kurt. "We really enjoy each other's company. Before, we'd be closer to friends than to each other. We couldn't say 'I love you' or give each other a hug up until a year ago. We became numb to each other."

"We were sick of living together and sharing everything. We got very guarded and weren't nice to each other. We were ready for our independence and privacy. I think we had lower self-esteem than our friends because we were always comparing ourselves to each other. And I felt incomplete when I was by myself—like I didn't have a formed personality because I was always with Kurt."

"Whenever Kyle was sick and I had to go to school alone, I'd feel totally self-conscious and

"We have finally realized that we can be individuals, thinking our own thoughts and forming our own opinions. We've never been closer."

always kind of auditioning, trying to get better parts. At one point I was really frustrated because I thought that the ballet mistress, who casts us for parts, couldn't tell us apart, and that it was keeping us from progressing. I finally told her about my concerns. Since then, every time she sees me, she makes a point of saying my name. It feels good."

"But we never were really competitive with each other," says Kurt.

"In ballet school, I think we started getting competitive," disagrees Kyle. "Sometimes I'd get vibes—I'd think, 'Is Kurt trying to show me up? Why is he standing in front of me?' And then I thought, 'What's going on? We should be competitive with everybody else, not each other.'"

Last year, Kyle and Kurt moved into separate apartments for the first time in their lives. Until this point, they had been sharing the same career, the same schedule, the same friends, and the same home. Ironically, this move was responsible for the deeper emotional closeness they now feel.

wouldn't know how to act. We latched onto each other like security blankets. Now, by getting our own places, we developed confidence and our own personalities."

"We have finally realized that we can be individuals, thinking our own thoughts and forming our own opinions. We've never been closer," smiles Kyle.

"I don't have to prove anything to him,"

affirms Kurt. "And he doesn't have to prove anything to me. We know where we stand, and we love each other."

Kyle adds, "I hate that whenever I turn on a talk show about twins, it's not realistic—'Oh, how cute, we're twins, we're dressing alike.' But that's just the way you were born. You're not a freak, so why sell yourself like that? It really bothers me when twins play up the physical part of it and don't talk about the closeness, which is what I want to stress."

The Fromans come from a long line of singers and dancers. Their grandmother was one of the original Rockettes; their mother was a dancer in Saint Louis; and their father was a singer. At the early age of five, Kyle and Kurt enrolled in tap, jazz, and ballet lessons at their sister's dance studio in Fort Worth, Texas.

"At age seven, we wanted to do jazz. We never really liked ballet—it was something our sister made us do to learn technique," laughs Kurt.

While auditioning for *The Nutcracker* at age eleven, they fell in love with ballet, and later joined their first professional ballet school, Fort Worth School of Ballet.

"We loved ballets by choreographer George Balanchine," remembers Kurt. "All the tapes that we had seen of his were with the New York City Ballet." After taking only six months of dance classes at the School of American Ballet in New York, the Fromans auditioned and were chosen to join the company at the age of twenty.

"We've been in a lot of ballets, including *Prodigal Son*, *Scotch Symphony*, and *Stars and Stripes*," Kurt says.

"It's great earning a living doing what you love—and being proud of what you do," smiles Kyle. "When we were young, school and ballet were two different worlds—we didn't want to stand out. But now that we're focused and living in New York, where there's a whole different energy and appreciation of the arts, people even recognize us on the street. They respect our hard work."

Kyle describes their demanding daily schedule. "I wake up around 8:00 every morning except for Mondays, our free day. We have to get to the theater around a quarter to 10:00 and start warming up for class. Usually class runs from 10:30 to 12:00. Then we have about four or five hours of rehearsal, usually between 12:00 and 6:00 P.M. After 6:00, we have an hour to eat. Then we usually get our makeup on at 7:00 and start warming up for the performances, which usually run from 8:00 to 11:00 P.M." They keep this grueling schedule for eleven months of the year.

When the schedule gets to be too much, Kurt and Kyle have each other for support. "When I get frustrated and think, 'I'd love to quit and go to school—or do something completely different,' at the same time I say to myself, 'How can I even be thinking this way?' I've achieved something I've always wanted to do. I do love it. I just get tired sometimes. I get burnt out," Kyle relates.

For now, Kyle and Kurt will continue pursuing their dreams and using their free time to grow intellectually. In a field where the average age for retirement is before forty, Kyle and Kurt have a similar plan for the future—"To do well in the company and be happy," says Kurt.

The brothers look at each other and smile. "Whatever happy is," Kyle laughs.

Jamillah Ali
Rasheda Ali-Walsh

"I think we're blessed," says twenty-seven-year-old Rasheda Ali-Walsh of her relationship with her sister, Jamillah Ali. "We love being twins. That's an understatement. It's really special—to have Jamillah to share my dark, deep secrets with."

"It's hard to explain to other people that Rasheda is not like a regular sister," adds Jamillah. "She's closer because she's like half of me. I love my other siblings dearly, but it's not the same. If Rasheda's not there, something's missing. That's not to say we never have an argument, but I can't stay mad at her."

Being twins has had a significant influence on Jamillah and Rasheda, as has being the daughters of Muhammad Ali, the three-time winner of the World Heavyweight Boxing Championship title.

With their father frequently on the road boxing, Rasheda and Jamillah were fortunate to have each other for support as children. They vividly recall childhood moments, sitting together and watching their father on TV.

"We would see him and say, 'Oh, that's neat, he's on TV.' But we didn't say, 'Get him Daddy.' We used to hate the fighter that hit him. We couldn't even watch it, because boxing is so violent. Imagine seeing someone hitting your father. Boxing is a sport, but when you're a child you don't know that. You just see someone hitting your father, and you don't like him."

Like the rest of the world, Rasheda and Jamillah have tremendous admiration for their father—his courage, his humanitarian efforts, and the values he instilled in them as individuals. They credit their father in large part for their own modesty.

"He was very humble," says Rasheda. "We didn't realize he was famous. We just realized he was popular. It wasn't a big deal because Daddy didn't make it a big deal. If Daddy seemed brash and conceited, it was just a marketing tool. He's

Jamillah Ali (left) and Rasheda Ali-Walsh visit their father, Muhammad Ali, on his farm in rural Michigan.

really not like that. To tease us, he would walk toward the mirror and say, 'Oooh, ain't I pretty?' He'd just say that to make us laugh."

Jamillah adds, "Daddy's so cool. We'd go to the gas station—and Daddy would get out and pump the gas. People would drive by and think that it couldn't be him. They'd say, 'That's not Muhammad Ali—not at a gas station pumping gas.' And that's why I think people more than love him—they admire him. They respect him. Because he's normal."

Rasheda and Jamillah, along with their older sister Maryum and younger brother Muhammad, moved from Philadelphia to Chicago in 1977. "My father was traveling and boxing. That was kind of his heyday. My mom went to L.A. to be an actress," explains Rasheda. "So, in 1977, my grandparents took us in and pretty much raised us as normal kids."

"My grandma's an angel," smiles Jamillah. "And my grandfather has been just as wonderful."

"When I was married in June at Biggs Restaurant, where my husband, Bob, works as a chef," Rasheda recounts, "both my father and my grandfather walked me down the aisle. I feel comfortable talking to Daddy about anything. Before I got married, we had a heart-to-heart. He asked, 'Does he treat you right? Is he good to you?' And he reminded me how marriage and family are really important in Islam."

Jamillah is pleased about Rasheda's happiness,

yet admits that sharing her sister's time is difficult. "When Rasheda first met Bob, she still spent time with me. But as she started spending more time with Bob, I was lonely all the time. So I bought a cat. I named him Hollywood. He loved me, and that's what I love. But it still isn't Rasheda. There's really no replacement. When she's not there, I'm lonely."

"Jamillah's always there for me," Rasheda declares, "but when she moved to Maryland, I felt guilty. I should have spent more time with her. Bob loves me a lot, and wants me to spend time with my family. He also wants to be with me when he's off work. He has to share and be more understanding about my time. He says he understands because he's really close with his sister, but I tell him he doesn't understand because he's not a twin."

Jamillah likes her brother-in-law—he makes her sister happy.

"I once had a boyfriend whom Jamillah hated," teases Rasheda. "I used to sneak out the window because she wouldn't let me go out with him. Jamillah once had a boyfriend who was mean to her, and I almost beat him up."

"I feel like whoever I'm going to be with, Rasheda has to approve, because, first, I trust her judgment," explains Jamillah. "Second, I'm not going to be in a good situation if I like that person and Rasheda doesn't. We're too close not to be together. If he doesn't like Rasheda, then there's something wrong with him in the first place, and I shouldn't be with him."

Jamillah, a single mother, recalls how Rasheda was there at the birth of her daughter, Nadia. "I needed her. If it weren't for Rasheda, I would have been depressed during my labor. Rasheda was there the whole time. When Nadia and I came home, Rasheda surprised me and had the whole nursery set up for me."

The experience was moving for Rasheda, too.

"I was in the delivery room. When I saw Nadia's little head, I started crying. I was so happy. The doctor asked, 'Are you okay?' I said, 'Yeah. She's the cutest thing I've ever seen.'"

"She's the best aunt for Nadia," Jamillah adds. "She treats Nadia as if she were her own. I know that if she ever has kids, I'll treat them like they're my own. I know Nadia's going to get a little jealous, but, you know."

Although Rasheda and Jamillah lived apart for two years, they now reside in Chicago and often meet for lunch. They intend to stay close, even if Rasheda, an actress, moves to Los Angeles.

"I wouldn't go unless I had a job for Jamillah," says Rasheda. "I can't leave her."

"I'd go with her in a heartbeat," responds Jamillah. Then she recalls with a laugh, "My grandparents say when we were little I followed behind her all the time like a little shadow. I look up to Rasheda because she's the first born. She always took more initiative than I did."

She continues, "We used to dress alike up until high school. We started hating the fact that people would always ask, 'Awwww, are you twins?' and stare at us. I felt like I was in a circus or something. I hated the 'Awwww.' So, at the point when we started hating it, we started dressing differently and taking different classes. We loved each other for who we were, but we wanted to be our own person at that point."

"People used to give us the same gifts or one to split," recalls Rasheda. "They used to cheat and get us one birthday card: 'Happy Birthday twins,' not Rasheda and Jamillah. It makes you say, 'Hey, we're two different people.'"

"When you're at that age when you're trying to establish who you are, you don't want people to always see you with your twin," Jamillah adds. "But then you get older and get over it—and you appreciate your twin. Now we say, 'Who cares?'"

"The only disadvantage of our twinship is the fear of something happening to Jamillah. When you love someone so much, it's devastating to think about it."

"The most tragic thing that could ever happen in my life is for anything to happen to Rasheda—or Nadia," Jamillah agrees. "It makes you say, 'Okay, I've got to deeply meditate and be a good person. Let me treat everybody nicely, because I don't want anything bad to happen to me or my

"I don't think any person should fight and stay mad at a loved one. Family is too important. Life is too short."

twin.' That would completely change my entire life and I'd never be the same. I don't think any person should fight and stay mad at a loved one. Family is too important. Life is too short. Most people don't want to swallow their pride and say, 'I'm sorry. Even though we disagree, I still love you.' You should appreciate every moment that you have with your twin or loved ones. The reasons why people fight and argue are so small compared to what life's plan is."

Scot Hollonbeck
Sean Hollonbeck

"July 20, 1984, was a defining moment in our twin relationship," explains twenty-eight-year-old Scot Hollonbeck of the incident that forced his path to diverge from his twin's. "I had just gotten a new bike, a Schwinn Super Le Tour II that I had picked up the night before. I was really excited about my first ride. So at 5:00 A.M., I jumped out of bed and gave Sean a kick. He said, 'I don't feel like going to swim practice today.' And I thought, 'You snooze, you lose.'"

This morning was rare, as the fourteen-year-old brothers usually went to swim practice together. "I had my bowl of Grape Nuts, gave my mom a kiss, and jumped on my bike down the two-lane country road," continues Scot. "I remember shifting gears, and that was it. When I woke up, I knew I had been hit by a car. The driver was allegedly drunk. I was in physical shock. I just remember lying there. It started to drizzle. I was more upset about my bike than

anything else. I had no clue what was going on. I had slid along the road for a decent way, so I had lost a lot of skin. My upper body was twisted the opposite way from my hips. The fire chief and my dad came out and were very calm. But when my mom came out—she took one look at me and lost it. And then it started to hit me that maybe this was a pretty serious situation."

Sean recalls that moment. "My family heard the accident because it was right by our house. My parents forbade me to go out to the site. When my dad came back he said, 'Scot's been hit. He's probably going to die. I'm going to the hospital.' Then they rushed off with the ambulance. My sister was away at theatrical camp, and my neighbors came to get my younger brother. I was left home all alone. I waited a good forty-five minutes, then I finally went outside. I started picking up bike pieces— broken spokes, torn-up rim. I can remember being really angry at myself for not being there

Scot (left) and Sean Hollonbeck take a break on Rural Road 7, after a twelve-mile workout in Columbus, Georgia.

for my brother, and punching the garage wall until my fist was all bloody. A million questions went through my mind. 'Why Scot? Why not me? What did he do to deserve this?' I felt a lot of remorse and guilt that I wasn't there."

It wasn't until mid-afternoon that a neighbor drove Sean to the trauma center where Scot was in surgery for about seven hours. When Scot awoke, he was in critical condition in an intensive care unit. No one was talking.

"I had some internal bleeding," Scot relates, "and my spinal column had been shattered, severing my spinal cord. The medical staff really didn't know what they were getting into. I could read the fear and uncertainty on their faces. I was pretty fortunate that I had just been baptized about nine days before—my faith in God really helped me through. That whole day was probably a lot harder on my twin, because he was left at home helpless and with no information. When it happens to you, your job's easy—just to survive." At the end of the day, the doctors told Scot that he was paralyzed from the waist down.

"We went day by day," Sean recalls. "The whole time I was left with a sense of emptiness, of not being able to contribute or help. That really got to me because I went from doing everything with Scot to boom I couldn't do a single thing with him. It just ate away at me. The biggest thing that helped was being able to see

my brother. He has always been very positive. From day one, he never let the accident get him down."

"I would wake up in the mornings and try to move my toe," Scot remembers. "It didn't work. That continual failure was depressing. But I didn't have a lot of time to be depressed because I felt like everybody around me was depressed. I realized that if the situation wasn't going to change, I had to change or something was going to give. I thought, 'Let's get going.' I couldn't stand seeing the fear and questions in their eyes, so I would always joke with everybody."

The fact that they were twins also offered the occasional lighter moment. Scot laughs as he recalls one day when "paramedics rolled me into the rehab center on a gurney. Sean walked in, but somehow they didn't see him at the front desk. Then six hours later Sean walked out. The lady at the desk fell back in her seat and exclaimed, 'Wow! That's the fastest recovery we've ever had!'"

But Scot admits that the ordeal was tremendously challenging. "One of the hardest parts for me wasn't when they said, 'You'll never walk again.' I could deal with that. The hard part for me was, 'You'll never run again, you'll never jump again, you'll never swim again.' When I got out of rehab, it was so difficult to watch on the sidelines—just like somebody stabbing you from the inside and the outside. One part of me was so excited for my brother when he made a tackle in football, but the other half looked at the wheelchair and got angry."

"I felt guilty sometimes," Sean recalls. "I obviously wanted Scot to be on the playing field, too. It hurt to see him watching. Especially in basketball, because Scot had been such an excellent basketball player. He learned to play wheelchair basketball and became very skilled at that, becoming the MVP for the University of Illinois for two years in a row, and the highest scorer one season. He was also on the winning Nationals team twice."

Scot's positive attitude helped him return to sports almost immediately. "It was really difficult when I came back. People looked at me and didn't know how to act toward me. Diane McNealy, my swim coach, was a phenomenal influence. When she visited me in the hospital, she didn't look at all the tubes or ask how I was doing. She just asked, 'When are you going to be back to practice? Ask your doctor when you can go into the pool. Then I expect to see you there.' And that's exactly what I needed. I didn't need sympathy or fear. I needed expectation."

"The best way to educate people is to put them in somebody else's shoes," says Sean.

insisting on being turned upright, I lay there watching in awe. Instead of seeing clunky wheelchairs like I had imagined life to be for me, I saw power, agility, strength, and fluidity of motion. I saw phenomenal athletes. I looked at my mom and said, 'That's what I want to do.'"

Back in school, Scot resumed training with the track team, but not without resistance. "Some high school track teams would cancel track meets rather than have Scot race," says Sean. "They would use all kinds of poor excuses. For example, my favorite one was, 'No wheeled vehicles are allowed on the track.' And then my coach said, 'If he can't race, the team won't go.' I was always really proud of him for that. My dad and Scot went to court over the issue of disabled

"Instead of seeing clunky wheelchairs like I had imagined life to be for me, I saw power, agility, strength, and fluidity of motion. I saw phenomenal athletes."

"There are some things you don't understand until you've tried them. My dad would take us to the mall and have us push around in a wheelchair to see what it was like for Scot. It was especially difficult at our school, which was rated one of the most inaccessible schools in the state of Illinois, with multiple levels and no elevators. It was a logistical nightmare for Scot to get around."

Fortunately, Scot found his focus early on. "Four days after the accident, I was doing floor time, which means I was staring at the floor from an inverted hospital bed that rotated every few hours. The 1984 Olympics happened to be on TV, and the announcer introduced the women's 800-meter wheelchair race. After

students participating in sports. The suit ended up going to the Illinois Supreme Court. We finally established the precedent giving every student the opportunity to participate in sports in the state of Illinois."

"It was the first civil rights case in America to address the issue of wheelchair participation in school sports," says Scot proudly. "Had I not been told that I couldn't be on the track team, I doubt if I would still be racing today. After my accident, I thought that everything to do with

being an athlete was over. Then I was competing again, and when somebody takes that from you again, you fight for it even more."

A year after the accident, Scot started seriously training for wheelchair racing, learning tactics, technique, and form. "The first six to eight years of race training were pretty difficult. I remember going to the preliminaries for the 1988 Paralympic Team. I got smoked—beaten by a minute in a four-minute race! So I didn't get to go to the Paralympics in Seoul, South Korea."

Inspired by swimmer Mark Spitz, he broke his goal down to manageable intervals. Since then, Scot has been a major force in both the Olympic Games, which has a 1500-meter wheelchair racing event, and the Paralympic Games. Sixty family members, nicknamed "Team Hollonbeck" in local newspapers, came to cheer him on during the 1996 Paralympic Games.

"I went to two Olympic games, where I was in the finals, and won a silver medal. And then I went to two Paralympic Games—where I won two golds and three silvers. I think that's the pinnacle. You hear the roar of the crowd. The challenge is trying to stay focused on what it is that you love—the pure emotion and the movement."

Scot has become a motivational speaker and an activist. In 1993, he helped start a nonprofit organization, Momentum International, to help people with disabilities throughout the world.

"The bottom line is, sports has been a great asset in my life," Scot says. "Now it's my mission to use sports to empower and educate people. Our goal is to have people see abilities rather than disabilities."

Scot's biggest supporter has been his brother, with whom he sometimes trains and who travels with him to many races. In 1993, Scot broke both his wrists during a race. "You talk about a twin helping out," says Scot. "Here I was, this professional wheelchair racer, with casts on my arms and having to start all over again. Sean took a leave from medical school to help me.

"If Sean had a disability, I would be there for him, try to understand, and try to educate myself about it. Twins always have someone to say, 'Look, I'm here to care about you. Whatever your struggle, however you decide to deal with it. It might take you five years to get over this, but guess what? I'll be there in three years. I'll be there in five. I'll be there for as long as it takes.'"

"We're part of each other," Sean explains, "and to see him accomplish his goals and be the best in the world just makes me glow. Since Scot's accident, I've spent half my time trying to teach people about what I've learned about disabilities. If a set of twins is placed in a challenging situation, they need to support each other, go on with their lives, and grow together into who they're going to be."

It was Scot's experience that inspired Sean to attend medical school. "When the accident occurred, I hated that feeling of being totally helpless and not knowing what to do. I made up my mind that I would never be in that position again."

Scot credits his twin for much of his success and drive. "I think every human being struggles to develop an identity. For a twin, it starts earlier. Once you are secure with yourself, it's easier to let people in. Being a twin helped prepare me for having a disability because I had to search for an identity at a very early age—to differentiate myself from Sean. People with disabilities have that same struggle in life. They say, 'Wait a minute, I'm an individual with these characteristics. Please take time to see that.'"

John Keach
Kristopher Keach

Jane Seymour's name conjures up many images—post-Civil War doctor Michaela Quinn on TV's *Dr. Quinn, Medicine Woman*, beautiful Clairol spokesperson, charity volunteer and international spokesperson for the United Nations International Children's Emergency Fund (UNICEF), and actress in many other TV shows and movies. But most important to her are her family roles as wife and mother of six children—most recently, two-year-old fraternal twins, Kristopher and John.

Kris and John like to visit the *Dr. Quinn* set. "They're on the set every day since they were about three months old," Jane says between takes. She sits on her wooden director's chair on the set in the sprawling foothills of Los Angeles. "Kristopher and John were talking yesterday. The first word out of Kris's mouth was 'Cut!' because that's what they say at the end of filming. And, Johnny's favorite word right now is 'Action!'"

Jane's enthusiasm as a mother of twins is evident in her voice and smile. "I had no idea what to expect. I thought, 'How wonderful, two for the price of one.' But it's more like having three. Two boys, they go in two different directions. You need three sets of hands!" Luckily, at age forty-six, Jane has the stamina and energy to keep up with her kids.

She does admit that having twins involves special challenges: "Just trying to make things fair all the time. Realizing that you do sometimes have to get two of something identical, even though it seems less cost-effective—and letting them know that they're both individuals and that they're loved as individuals. The fact that they were born at the same time is remarkable and special, but they're also both special in their own right—whether they are twins or not.

"While Johnny listens to people and likes to build things and clean things up, Kristopher likes to knock them over and pull all the books off the

Jane Seymour spends time with sons Kristopher (left) and John Keach on their private beach in Malibu, California.

shelves! John constantly loves to be hugged and cuddled and held, whereas Kris is always on the move, looking for new adventures. Kristopher is an athlete and naturally throws a ball, hits things, runs. He'll do everything about two or three weeks before John does. Krissy will ride a horse, then Johnny will ride a horse. Krissy will hit the ball, then Johnny will hit the ball.

"They both love to dance," Jane continues, as she swings a smiling Kris around her hip and dips him upside down. "He's my little 'Piglet,' and I call John 'Pooh.'" Kris is named after Jane's good friend and source of inspiration Christopher Reeve, her leading man in the romantic movie *Somewhere in Time*. John was named after friend Johnny Cash as well as Jane's father, Dr. John Frankenberg.

Parenting twins inspired Jane and her husband, actor and director James

has to be told off—exactly the same—and be given the same punishment."

"I have double love every morning and every night when I get kissed goodnight," James jokes.

"They have a built-in playmate, which is absolutely fantastic," smiles Jane. "They hold hands to go places, and they put themselves to bed at night. They decide it's bedtime, take their bottles, and start walking to their cribs. They say, 'Night, night,' and that's it."

"At night," says James, "when we have the baby monitor on, they talk for a long time in a language that only they understand."

"In the morning they have long conversations before we come and pick them up. They don't just wake up and want to get out of bed," Jane notes. "They've gone to preschool much earlier

"I had no idea what to expect. I thought, 'How wonderful, two for the price of one.' But it's more like having three."

Keach, to write a children's book, *This One and That One*. "It's the true story of these guys," James says. "It's their adventures in life, along with those of our other children."

"When they were in my tummy," Jane explains, "everyone would say, 'This one moves more than that one.' And when they were born, 'This one has more hair than that one,' or 'This one's bigger than that one.' They were always 'This one' and 'That one.' For the book, we made 'This one' and 'That one' two little kittens growing up at the same time.

"We have spoken to lots of twins to ask their advice. They tell me you have to do things differently and independently with twins—dress them differently, let them have their own individual time and space. Yet Kristopher and John want everything the same. They love each other, but they also fight for everything. If one has something, the other one has to have it, too. If I pick one up, the other one has to be picked up. At thirty-two pounds apiece, that's pretty heavy! Even if one gets told off, the other

than other kids and are way ahead in terms of being social, because they always have another one to learn from. They understand sharing well. Some of the first words that came out of their mouths were 'my turn.'

"It was interesting, instead of calling me Mommy, they call me 'Mom-mee,' and we wondered why that came about. Then we realized that what they were saying was 'Mom, me! Me! Not him—me!'"

Mark Kelly
Scott Kelly

Thirty-three-year-old Scott and Mark Kelly are the first identical twins—in fact, the first blood relatives—in history to be selected for NASA's astronaut corps of less than three hundred people. There have been astronauts with twin siblings before—Charlie Duke, who walked on the moon in 1972, has a twin brother, as does Joe Tanner, who participated in the 1997 Hubble telescope repair mission. But never before had *both* twins become NASA astronauts—until the Kellys were accepted into the NASA class of 1996.

Mark and Scott trained for four years at different colleges to become Navy pilots, wound up in the same class at test pilot school, and excelled academically and professionally while separated for the next ten years. Then they decided to apply to NASA to become astronauts, and they went through the rigorous process of written applications, medical exams, a week-long interview, and a week-long physical.

They wore the same suit for each of their interviews, with Mark's occurring a month before Scott's.

"I didn't have a nice suit at the time," Mark laughs, "so I borrowed Scott's!"

"When I got the acceptance phone call from senior astronaut Dave Leestma," Scott recalls, "I was very excited. He told me he had just talked to my brother. I thanked him and then tried to call our relatives, but Mark was obviously ahead of me, because the number of every person I called was busy."

"When I heard that Scott was accepted, I was almost as happy as when I found out that I made it! Not quite as much, but almost," Mark grins.

"The Navy didn't even know we were twins until we showed up on the same day for training at test pilot school," Scott exclaims. "It really wasn't something that we planned or discussed much. But we had the same interests and by default participated in the same things. Most

Scott (left) and Mark Kelly stand inside the engine of a Saturn V rocket at Johnson Space Center, Houston.

military test pilots apply to be astronauts—it's kind of a logical progression."

Mark and Scott train at the Johnson Space Center in Houston, practicing shuttle landings in simulators and attending lectures on topics ranging from orbital mechanics and navigation to the best ways to eat and sleep while weightless. They undergo a rigorous exercise program and a course in survival skills. Before they fly their first mission in space as pilots, they will be required to have at least five hundred simulated shuttle landings—and to become commanders, they will need to have one thousand such landings. While the brothers see each other every day for training, they describe themselves as being very independent.

"We're not into the twin thing," admits Mark. "Neither of us is very touchy-feely. I don't think we rely much on each other's support or are very competitive with each other. My wife, Amy, is a twin; she's the only twin I know."

"People used to ask me why I didn't marry Amy's twin," adds Scott with a smile. "What I'd tell them was, I wasn't very interested in Bill—he's her fraternal twin."

"The best part about being a twin is that you have spare organs!" Mark jokes, quickly adding, "I'm just kidding. As kids, Scott and I spent time together just like any two brothers would if they were close in age. We had fistfights

every single day from the time we could move until we were about fifteen."

"A slugfest," admits Scott. "These fights would go on for hours and were pretty exhausting. We'd finally realize it was futile, and that was it."

"It just went away one day," says Mark. "I think we started to grow up."

.   .   .

"Our families are used to a little bit of risk in our daily lives," Scott notes: their parents are retired police officers, their father was a paratrooper in the Army, and both grandfathers fought in World War II.

"I loved flying F-14s," says Scott. "Landing a Navy plane on an aircraft carrier at night is probably one of the most dangerous jobs around—it's in the back of your mind during the entire flight. You're in this big, black void in an airplane going well over one hundred miles an hour, flying toward the water, with the ship moving up and down and away from you at the same time. You have to find the ship and then land on an area angled away from you that's less than two hundred feet wide and about five hundred feet long."

"My biggest experience as a pilot was flying in Desert Storm, November 1990 to April 1991," Mark relates of his thirty-nine combat missions. "I almost got shot down a few times over the Persian Gulf. I had a couple of missiles shot at me one night, and one of them detonated near my airplane."

"I was in Virginia Beach sitting on the couch watching the whole war on CNN," says Scott. "I thought about Mark being over there, and was concerned. But I knew he was a very well-trained Navy pilot and could take care of himself."

While Scott and Mark are very independent, they have always made for a strong team from their early years as co-captains of their high

eventually landing a real space shuttle. "The space shuttle's a rocket ship until it gets into orbit; then it's a space ship. When it comes back to earth, it's basically a big lumbering airplane, no engines," Mark explains. "And unlike flying an airplane, you only get one shot at landing. When it decides, somewhere over the Indian Ocean, that it's going to come home, it fires engines to get out of orbit, and it's committed to flying halfway around the world to Florida and gliding back to earth unpowered, at a very steep angle, to land."

Initially, many members of their NASA class had a hard time telling the Kellys apart.

"I shower more often," Scott laughs.

Their classmates have learned the differences

"The Navy didn't even know we were twins until we showed up on the same day for training at test pilot school."

school swim team to the present when they fly NASA's T-38 jets together.

"In the cockpit," Mark explains, "there's a division of responsibilities called crew coordination. Every time you fly with someone new, you notice whether you work well together or not. When I fly with Scott, we do very well— no matter who's sitting in the front seat and who's in the back. We're a better team than anyone else I might fly with. I think it's from knowing each other so well."

The Kellys' carrier experience was great training for a similar but more complicated challenge: performing shuttle-type landings in simulators and shuttle training aircraft, and

in their personalities—or they make a point of getting close enough to read the names on their identification badges.

"We find people occasionally glancing down at our name tags to tell us apart," says Mark, "but almost everybody in our class can tell us apart now."

Although the Kellys work and train hard, they try to spend as much time as they can with their families. Both are married. Mark has two daughters, and Scott has one. While their wives don't have trouble telling them apart, their children used to.

"When my daughter was about two, she used to confuse her Uncle Scott for me," Mark remembers.

Talking about their children spurs the brothers' memories of their own childhood—and the moment they first dreamed of becoming astronauts.

"I remember Neil Armstrong taking that first step on the moon," Scott says. Their parents got them out of bed to watch the historic event on TV in 1969.

They also recall watching Alan Shepard as commander of an Apollo mission to the moon in 1971. "Both he and Neil Armstrong were Navy pilots before they became astronauts, and that stuck in the back of my mind," states Mark.

• • •

"This unique and exciting opportunity to serve our country, if not people all over the world, is really important," Scott says. "And every day is different, not routine at all. It's really an honor to work with all of the capable people that support the space program."

"Over the last thirty years," Mark enthuses, "the space program has provided our planet with huge advancements in material science, medicine, computers, space science, and earth observations that directly impact the conditions of our lives and environment. In the future, with the International Space Station being assembled, I think we're going to see a great amount of technological advancement. Ultimately we're going to go back to the moon and then eventually put people on Mars."

Both brothers have goals to fly successful missions as pilots and commanders of the space shuttle. "And whatever missions follow," Mark adds—such as going to Mars or back to the moon, fixing the Hubble space telescope, spending time on Mir (Russia's orbiting outpost), or working on the planned International Space Station.

"We'll probably fly our first mission in two to three years," Scott predicts, explaining that he and his twin will probably not fly the same mission due to their similar experience and position as pilots. "I think the future of the space program is really bright," he adds. "From the Wright brothers' first flight in 1903, it was just sixty-six years until man stepped foot on the moon. So in the next sixty-six years, think of what we can accomplish if we really put our minds to it. Our potential is limitless!"

Jeannine Bobardt
Denise North

"—beep—Denise, it's time!
Your babies are being delivered!"

Denise North and her husband, Kevin, listened to the answering machine in disbelief and anticipation. It was only November 24—the babies were four weeks earlier than expected! The ensuing two-hour drive seemed like eternity as they sped from San Diego to Los Angeles's Glendale Adventist Hospital where their babies—triplets—had just been delivered. They rushed to the room where Jeannine Bobardt, Denise's fraternal twin sister and surrogate mother to Denise's babies, was resting after the deliveries.

"When Kevin and I arrived at the hospital," says Denise, "we went directly to Jeannine's room to see how she was doing." Next, Denise went to see her babies, and she felt an immediate motherly bond. "At first I was scared when I saw the babies being monitored in the NICU [Neonatal Intensive Care Unit]. Then I was so happy and excited to see that they were healthy. It was very emotional—I started to cry."

"I was given this gift of a healthy body and I just felt I had to share it. It wasn't Denise's fault that she ended up being sick. It could have been me," says Jeannine. "She never asked me to do it. How could you ask somebody to be a surrogate? I just wanted to make her happy."

Jeannine knows that she will always be an integral part of her sister's life, as well as the lives of her new niece, Elise, and nephews Adam and Joshua. Jeannine's children, six-year-old Evan and three-year-old Sarah, are as intrigued by and adoring of their new cousins as their mom is.

As thirty-five-year-old Denise and Jeannine relate their story, their four hands methodically lift the babies into their three matching highchairs where they will drink from the Podee system—a new apparatus specially designed for multiple birth children. The individual bottles are attached by long straw-like tubes to rubber

Jeannine Bobardt (left) and Denise North hold Denise's triplets, Adam, Elise, and Joshua near San Diego, California.

nipples, allowing mom more freedom with her hands. The babies' light hair and skin stand out against their blue denim outfits—a dress for Elise, and matching pantsuits for Joshua and Adam.

"I thought I was pregnant before Jeannine was, even though she got married nine years earlier," explains Denise. "But it was a false alarm. It turned out that I was having a lot of medical problems with my uterus. My doctor at that time told me, 'You will probably never have children.' I had uterine fibroid cysts which were too numerous to control."

Meanwhile, Jeannine and her husband, Dave, decided to have children; they had no problems starting a family. "The first time we didn't use birth control, I got pregnant," she laughs. Evan was born in 1991 and Sarah in 1994. Denise was sincerely happy for her sister, but she was also suffering.

"I was trying everything to conceive—medication to shrink the fibroids, hormones prescribed by infertility experts, even surgeries to remove dozens of cysts—only to have them grow back." Each time she thought she was pregnant, her hopes were shattered.

"It was like a roller coaster. She was constantly thinking about it for nearly five years," Jeannine recalls.

The stress of the situation was taking a toll on Denise and her marriage. Jeannine shared her sister's pain but could not relieve her suffering.

"They finally told me I needed a hysterectomy, and I agreed because I got to a point where I couldn't take it any longer," Denise says with resignation. "We wanted children desperately, but you have to draw the line somewhere. I was going crazy. I was constantly sick for five years—bleeding, anemic, and in pain."

Denise's happiness became a priority for Jeannine, who did what many people would never think of doing. "That first time the doctor told her that she may never have children I asked my husband, 'What would you think if I became a surrogate for her?' At that time, I had never even carried my own children yet. So, I put the idea out there. It was just a thought in my mind.

"When my daughter was a few months old, I told my obstetrician that my sister was going to end up having a hysterectomy," continues Jeannine. "And she said, 'You would be the perfect candidate to be a surrogate for her.' With a professional telling me that and knowing my body, it reassured me. I started doing some research."

Although Jeannine's husband was supportive of the idea, Denise started looking into other options, such as adoption. "But my husband and I were skeptical about adoption," says Denise. "And the cost of trying in vitro fertilization one time would be equal to or less than that of adoption, so we wanted to give it a try."

"I started really promoting surrogacy with her because she wouldn't ask me," adds Jeannine.

Joshua interrupts the conversation by rattling a toy in front of the others until it comes crashing to the floor. Elise and Adam stop drinking and smile with glee, their blue eyes bright with excitement. Denise smiles. "He loves the attention. He's the instigator. He's a ham. He'll scream just to hear himself scream. But they all love the same amount of attention. They get a little jealous sometimes when you're paying too much attention to one or the other."

"It is amazing how Elise is a spitting image of Denise." Denise beams as Jeannine reminds her of the many traits the kids have inherited from her.

Jeannine is content with Denise's updates about the babies. "For me, I am just thrilled. They're like little jewels that she is giving me when she calls and says, 'Adam rolled over for the first time.' All that day and night I'm thinking, 'Adam rolled over,' I can just see him. That's all I need."

From the beginning, Denise and Jeannine knew they made the right decision in choosing conviction. "First they had to get our systems coordinated with hormones," explains Denise, describing the process through which the needle-phobic Jeannine had to endure more than eighty injections in three months. Out of the thirteen eggs that were removed from Denise and joined with Kevin's sperm, only three would grow, divide, multiply, and survive to the next stage over the next four days.

Then they faced another dilemma. How many of the fertilized eggs should be implanted?

"We had done a lot of research and decided that we would put in all three to increase the small chance of having just one," recalls Jeannine.

"I was given this gift of a healthy body and I just felt I had to share it. It wasn't Denise's fault that she ended up being sick. It could have been me."

surrogacy. But it took time for others to share their enthusiasm. "Even our parents thought we were crazy at first," says Jeannine. "And now, they're just so supportive."

Dave, Jeannine's husband, was very supportive, considering it a tremendous act of sisterly love. At first, Denise's husband, Kevin, felt it was too much to ask, and that the option of using his sperm but Jeannine's eggs would cause too much emotional and marital conflict. They ultimately decided to fertilize Denise's eggs with Kevin's sperm, then implant the cells into Jeannine. "And still some people don't understand that the babies are her and her husband's total biological children," Jeannine says with disbelief.

Both sisters would endure emotional and physical pain, but their love fueled their

"And if there was a slim chance of having twins, that was okay, because this was Denise's only chance of having children. But when we asked Kevin, he said, 'No, just put in two because if anyone will have triplets, it will be you.'"

"But when we were in the hospital," continues Denise, "the doctor said, 'I have never gotten anyone pregnant with even one baby by only putting in two.' So we panicked. The chances of all three of these taking were so, so, so slim, it was less than one percent. And we went ahead with the doctor's advice and put in three eggs. She had us so worried that we truly thought that

it wasn't going to work. We had read that there's only a fifteen percent chance of an in vitro working the first time. So I was on pins and needles."

Everyone tried not to get their hopes up as Jeannine lay flat on her back for forty-eight hours. She took the blood tests two weeks later.

"I wouldn't have done it again. I just figured, if it's meant to be, it's going to happen the first time," Denise says.

They wouldn't know for sure until the phone call came two weeks after the tests.

"I was crying on the phone," recalls Jeannine. "I couldn't believe it. The hormone level was so high that they thought it might be a multiple birth. But I never dreamed that they were triplets until I saw them on the sonogram at week four. Denise was thrilled but also worried about my physical health and the financial situation. I wasn't excited that I was going to have a Cesarean. And when I read that you will and should gain 50 to 75 pounds, I wanted to die."

Jeannine's daughter, Sarah, wasn't thrilled either, and started acting up at preschool. "She thought she was being replaced. But when she finally understood that they were Aunt Neesie's babies and would go back to San Diego with her, she was relieved. And now she loves them so much. She wants to come down to San Diego all the time."

Jeannine continues, "People would ask me how I could do it, but when you see Denise, and how Sarah and Evan love her so much . . . why couldn't I have that relationship with the babies? During the whole time I was pregnant with the triplets I maintained a completely different frame of mind than when I was pregnant with my own children. I dealt with it on a daily basis, but I just knew that these weren't going to be my babies. If I bought anything for them, I would just give it to Denise. And my husband would joke, 'My wife's pregnant. I'm going to be an uncle!'"

Denise quit her job toward the end of Jeannine's pregnancy in late October to spend weekdays caring for Jeannine and her family. Their mother, Adeline, took over on weekends.

The exciting call came four weeks earlier than expected. "They were supposed to be Christmas babies, but instead were Thanksgiving babies. They rushed me in for an emergency C-section." Jeannine barely had time to call her husband, who left a message for Denise and Kevin and hurried to be by Jeannine's side. "My husband said, 'Oh, they're big. They're beautiful. They're fine.' And then I was just so relieved for Denise." Jeannine pauses and admits, "I didn't really know how I was going to react, if I was going to feel like a mother toward them." The real test would come the following day. "I was holding Elise and she started crying. And my first reaction was to hand her to Denise. I was really relieved that I felt that way."

Perhaps the most difficult part came when Denise and the babies left the hospital to go back to San Diego. "Denise and I just suddenly started crying because we had gotten so close. I was so depressed and my husband didn't understand why. He thought it was because the babies were leaving. He didn't understand that Denise and I were being ripped apart again," Jeannine recalls with tears in her eyes.

Before leaving, Kevin reassured Jeannine that the babies would know what their special aunt did for them and their parents. "He said that there's a special place in heaven for me. I never did it for that—I was only thinking of making my sister happy."

Brady Ralston
Brian Ralston

"One of the first things that I tell people is, 'We're identical twins.' And then I always like throwing in, 'And—he's gay, and I'm straight,'" says twenty-eight-year-old Brian Ralston about his twin, Brady. "People are kind of blown away. There's a fascination with our different sexual orientations and our being twins."

"I've always known that I was gay," says Brady—"ever since I was a little kid. I never shared it with anybody except my parents, until after high school. A lot of our mannerisms, our laugh, and facial expressions are exactly the same. But Brian always had his own interests, and I always had mine, and that's what really set us apart. We were completely different but we looked exactly the same."

"We're pretty much like black and white," Brian agrees. "Brady's very artistic—into singing and dancing. And I love sports. Brady was in theater, often playing the lead. He was terrible at sports, but he was the best dancer, better than the girls. In fact, he was the first male cheerleader in our high school. And I played basketball on the varsity basketball team."

"Yeah, that was kind of the catch," laughs Brady. "I was pegged in high school as gay, but my brother always stood up for me."

"I stood up for him, and all my friends would stand up for Brady. I didn't think that he was gay because Brady and I are pretty close. I thought that he would have told me."

But Brady didn't come out to his identical twin until they were nineteen, even though he had told his parents at age fourteen.

"I was being harassed at school, so I wanted my parents to know. My mom and I talked about how my life would be different from Brian's. It was left up to me to tell people in my own time. They said that whenever the time was right for me to come out to Brian, I would."

Brady (left) and Brian Ralston spend time together at Golden Gate Park, San Francisco.

Brian seems to understand. "Back then, there was a lot of homophobia in our town. Brady would be teased by a handful of people, but everyone else just loved him for who he was, how crazy he was, and what a good actor he was. At the time we graduated from high school in 1988, people were becoming more aware of AIDS, that's when my mom first told me about Brady being gay. I was concerned and said, 'Okay, great, just as long as he's safe.' Then, about a week later, my dad told me. I was pissed that I was the last person to find out. I guess I didn't really open my eyes and see the big picture."

"I was still afraid of being rejected," Brady admits. "I never thought that Brian would totally reject me, but I didn't want to be put in that position. I was still fighting with myself, trying to come out to myself completely. Being gay and growing up without any role models back in the eighties, dealing with homophobia—it takes a long time to be comfortable with who you are. I was afraid that my twin wasn't going to like me, or just wouldn't understand. Probably because we were so close."

"And we were," Brian affirms. "We've always been really close. Always together."

"There's so much that makes up a person besides their sexual orientation," says Brady. "At nineteen, when I really came out, I was more confident in who I was. I decided that I would tell Brian. That it would be okay."

"But you didn't come out and tell me. I had to confront you," Brian reminds his brother.

"I was going to," Brady says defensively. "For the first year after we graduated from high school, Brian was traveling around the world teaching tennis at all-inclusive resorts like Club Med, and that was an easy excuse."

"When I returned home to visit for a couple of months, Brady and I were playing pool. I said, 'I know that you're gay. I love you. I just want you to be safe and be careful.' And that was it. He turned beet red and didn't say anything for a little while."

"I was pretty moved by Brian's being really cool about it. And I think what really touched me was his concern about being safe—he said that he didn't want me to die. So I had to give him a little update, that I wasn't the only one—he also needed to be safe," states Brady, who currently works for the Center for AIDS Prevention Studies at the University of California, San Francisco. He plans to become a psychologist specializing in gay and lesbian relationship issues.

Brady and Brian have grown even closer through the experience.

"It's a process," relates Brady. "It was a process for me to come out. It's a process for my family and Brian to become comfortable. And they are. I'm really fortunate."

After Brady came out, Brian continued to travel and teach tennis around the world for the next five years.

"In the past three years since my return, we've really gotten to know each other," adds Brian. "When I first came back from overseas, we had to reconnect. Now it's like we were when we were growing up."

"It's interesting to watch us get older and share similar life experiences with relationships and careers," remarks Brady. "To know that Brian's always there for me, and I'm there for him—that gets stronger as the years go on. I've come crying to Brian after a break-up with my boyfriend, and he's cried to me after a break-up with his girlfriend. We were pretty amazed that our relationships were very similar in the problems we were dealing with."

"I love telling people about my brother," Brian says warmly. "I always want my friends to meet my other half."

"My being gay opens up his world to a little more diversity," Brady says. "And it makes both of our lives richer. I feel very fortunate to have a straight brother. I like being the only gay one—the one really strong difference between us. That adds another special bond besides the twin thing.

"Everybody lays this big twin question on

could also move the gay population forward in receiving equal rights. On the negative side, I could imagine some people aborting babies if a test determined that their newborn was going to be gay. That really scares me.

"My brother and I may be different in who we choose to love intimately, but we share all of the same life problems. The great thing is, we accept each other for who we are, and that makes life so much more rewarding. I don'tcare what made Brian straight. And I know he doesn't care what made me gay. We just loveand care about each other. It's that simple."

"I think it comes down to education—and education on twins, too," says Brian. "We want to

"My brother and I may be different in who we choose to love intimately, but we share all of the same life problems."

you, expecting you to live up to some kind of a twin etiquette," continues Brady. "Like we're supposed to say, 'Oh yeah, we're exactly alike, and I feel everything he feels, and he's my best friend in the whole wide world, and. . . .' A lot of those things are true about us, but we really don't focus on that. We focus on who we've both become as people.

"People are fascinated by whether being gay is genetic or environmental. I think you really can't tell. You're given something genetically, then the environment and parenting play a dual role in how an individual is structured. I don't know. This is who I've always been. I'm scared to think what would happen if a gay gene was discovered. It could have some positive effects—it could dismiss the myth that being gay is a 'choice.' It

express how much fun it is being a twin and that twins are not all the same."

"We really care about the differences of who we are," interjects Brady. "The challenge is trying to break down the perception that all twins are exactly the same. I think that challenge instantly goes away once people meet us, because they see how different we are, and how similar, too."

"Yeah, I think that is it—right on the nail, Brady."

Ali and Jeff Stanch
Cal and Jim Stanch

Mr. McGregor proudly escorted his twin daughters on either arm down the aisle to meet their future husbands, also identical twins.

Cal and Ali, twenty-five-year-old twin nurses from Pennsylvania, had had no idea what was in store for them at the 1995 Twinsburg Twin Festival in Ohio. But when friends introduced them to twenty-nine-year-old Jim and Jeff Stanch from New Jersey, they knew things would change. Within the year, they would be saying their vows at their double marriage ceremony and living together under one roof.

"Living in the same house is actually easy because we all get along well," explains Ali.

"It's the understanding that we all have. There's no competition and no sense of a struggle relationship-wise," Jim describes.

The newlyweds returned from their honeymoon in the Poconos, where they had been dismayed by remarks from other vacationers.

"Some people asked the stupidest questions," Cal explains. "One couple had the nerve to ask us if we all shared a room on our honeymoon."

"We couldn't believe it," Ali says. "But the most annoying one of all was, 'Do you switch?'"

"We do a lot together, but there are some things that are private," Jim says firmly.

"We have the utmost respect for each other. We knock. We don't just barge in," Cal adds.

Both couples agreed that they would like to raise their families in separate houses, although down the block from one another. Cal says, "If we did have kids, it would be nice to have them around the same time."

"It would be great if they had one and we had one," Ali agrees. "They would be an only child but they would always have each other."

Both couples agree that their pairing off fell into place perfectly.

"It was just a magnetic thing. It wasn't like, 'which one do you want?—I'll take him and you take him.' It was natural," Cal declares. "The first born married the first born, and the second born married the second born."

"Before, Jeff and I were a team," Jim explains. "We still are, but now the team's just bigger. The four of us are a team. And the two of us—Cal and I—are a real strong team."

Jeff concludes, "We have our individuality but we have the same kind of commitment and devotion to our marital relationships as to our twins."

Cal and Jim Stanch (left) and Ali and Jeff Stanch pause for a photo at their wedding in Erie, Pennsylvania.

Brian McMullin
Donald McMullin

"Donald, don't leave me! Don't die! Stay with me!" Brian McMullin pounded on his fraternal twin brother's chest. "Officer shot! Officer shot! Donald, fight! Don't go on me yet!"

In a mere second, on the night of June 27, 1991, the lives of Brian and Donald McMullin were turned upside down. The twin brothers, then twenty-three years old, were working together as policemen in the 18th Police District in West Philadelphia, when they routinely stopped a car without a headlight. "There was something weird about the car," Brian recalls. "The three guys inside weren't looking at us. It just seemed eerie."

Donald and Brian got out of their patrol wagon. "Donald approached on the driver's side," Brian continues, "while I took the passenger's side." But something went terribly wrong. One of the passengers suddenly fired at Donald at point-blank range. Another fired at Brian, who in turn emptied all sixteen rounds from his 9-mm semiautomatic into the back of the fleeing car. The car reversed, crashed into their police wagon, then screeched off.

"Everything happened so fast. I didn't remember seeing Donald anymore. I started wondering if something went wrong. I remember thinking, 'Why isn't he shooting? Where is he?' I had the weird feeling that he got shot—that he wasn't alive—because I know he would have been backing me up then."

Donald was lying motionless in the middle of the road. Brian ran to his side. "I didn't bother reloading my gun. I didn't really care if I died. It was weird—I never thought I could feel that way about my life. I couldn't picture life without Donald. I just started crying and yelling at him to stay alive, not to leave—to stay with me. I saw blood come out of his eye. I was shaking him. He was just lifeless, he was white.

Donald (left) and Brian McMullin return to West Philadelphia, where Donald was shot.

I remember feeling his face. It was frozen—he just looked dead to me.

"I started CPR, called on the radio for an officer assist, and continued CPR until backup arrived and we got to Misericordia Hospital." Brian describes the ride as bumpy—their police wagon had one tire shot out in the gunfire.

Donald breaks the tension with humor. "I remember Brian performing CPR because I had my bullet-proof vest on, and they really weren't perfect compressions. You can't give chest compressions with a vest on, you've got to take the vest off first."

Donald had been barely clinging to life, but gave his brother one glimpse of hope. "After they put him on a stretcher at the hospital, Donald pushed my hand away and said, 'I'm not going to leave you.' That gave me hope. I think I was annoying him, actually, because of the chest compressions."

Donald recalls little of that night except the one thing that kept him going. "I remember Brian's voice. He was yelling, screaming, really frantic, 'Donald, don't leave me! Don't leave me, Donald!' Constantly. And I was trying to tell him, 'I'm not going to leave you.' But the words weren't coming out."

"I couldn't believe this was happening," Brian recollects. "I kept thinking, 'It's got to be a dream.'" Ironically, the brothers had discussed the possibility of such an encounter that very evening. "And then five minutes later . . ." Brian's voice trails off.

"We had a feeling we were going to be involved in a shooting sometime soon because we were making a lot of arrests and were hitting too many drug corners," Donald explains. "But we didn't have that fear because we didn't really know what it was like. I think the bullet-proof vest kind of gives you a false hope, too."

The bullet had entered Donald's skull next to his right eye and lodged in the occipital lobe in the back of his brain, the area that controls vision.

Brian was there by his brother's side on the long road to recovery. Donald endured life-threatening swelling in his brain, intense fevers, and surgery to remove dead brain tissue.

Then, a dreaded moment arrived. Brian was asked to say goodbye to his brother because Donald wasn't expected to survive the next surgery. "We had to sign papers. My mother was trying to get me to be realistic, telling me that Donald was probably going to die, that he was going to be with my grandfather. I just couldn't see that. I could not see that."

But the surgery was a success, and Donald kept fighting. Brian and his family began to consider how much brain damage and eyesight impairment Donald would have. "We didn't really care, as long as he was alive. We resigned ourselves that there was going to be a major change in our lives. And as long as he was alive, I was fine with that."

Donald didn't realize how much had changed until he was transferred to a rehabilitation center two and a half weeks after the shooting. "Donald amazed everybody by checking himself in. He didn't think he had a visual problem until they challenged him. He was bumping into objects," Brian recollects. "He had no peripheral vision—he didn't even have much vision straight ahead."

"It's all a matter of survival, it really is," Donald says. "If you really want to do it, you've just got to do it. I had to learn how to walk again because I was in bed for so long."

Things are slowly returning to normal in the brothers' lives, although

Donald and Brian are unable to return to their work as policemen—Donald for physical reasons, and Brian for psychological ones. Many other things have changed since the shooting. But one thing remains the same—the brothers' deep and constant devotion to each other. "I think the near-death experience made me think differently about life—that the little things aren't as important," Brian speculates. "My brother and I used to bicker over little things, and I can't even

find yourself wanting to just be with your twin. The way we were, we could have had no friends. We would have been happy with just the two of us."

"Some people feel that it's not healthy for twins to be together all the time. But, if we have fun doing something together, why not? I mean, I could see if we wound up divorcing our wives so we could be together, then there's something wrong. There's got to be something that cuts the cord," Donald explains. "We can go on in our separate lives and still be great brothers at the same time. We don't have to live in the same house.

But, Donald continues, "I think twins are different than just regular brothers. I figure,

"We're so close, that if one died, the other would
probably have died of a broken heart," Brian says.

do that now. It's just not important. I can't say it brought us closer together because we were always very close. It just made me realize how close we really are."

Now, after thirty years of sharing every moment of their lives, Brian and Donald have also realized their individual needs. Because the gunmen were apprehended, the brothers have had closure on the experience and are now going in separate directions. They both married recently and now live in different cities.

"I think it's healthy going our own ways," says Donald. "Before, it was like we were one person. We always talked about ourselves plurally, like, 'We're doing this . . .' I think it's great for parents to try to give twins individualism."

"It's tough as a twin," adds Brian. "You still

we were born in the same womb, where for nine months we were in a cramped space. We had to get to know each other. We had to like each other. We had no choice in that!" he laughs. Then, more seriously, he adds, "Maybe when we were growing up we should have been separated more because we're so close."

"We're so close, that if one died, the other would probably have died of a broken heart," Brian says. "I was not ready for Donald to die. It was pretty much, 'If you go, I go.' I couldn't picture life without him."

Amina Kurtovic
Azra Kurtovic

"When the war started in Bosnia in 1992, Amina and I were basically grounded, living in our basement for about a year and a half," recalls seventeen-year-old Azra Kurtovic about the life that she and her fraternal twin sister, Amina, had shared. "It was hard. We didn't have water or electricity. The schools stopped working. Our apartments were constantly being shelled. There were always soldiers on the streets coming back from the front lines. In 1994, we got electricity back but it was restricted to one hour a day, and we had running water for only two hours a day. Everything was on and off depending on how often we were shelled. We ate food that we had stored in preparation for the war, but in 1993, we ran out of everything, so we ate the basics—beans, beef, and rice. After a year, we got used to the shells, so that when there were no shells, we wondered if something was wrong."

"Waiting was worse than actually knowing that the shells were being sent," adds Amina.

"We were extremely lucky to have one another. Most of the other kids were not as close with their siblings because they were different ages, whereas Amina and I were always together," says Azra.

"Most of the time," Amina recalls, "I would read or talk to Azra and my friends who lived in the same apartment building. We would play games like Monopoly. Sometimes when it was calm, our mom would let us go in front of the building. But she wouldn't let us go far.

"It was really dangerous to go out into the streets, especially for the first two years of the war. For a few weeks, they would shell every hour on the hour. Walking home from school or work was like a psychological game with the enemy," explains Amina, thankful that their mother, Sabira, survived her daily walks to a nearby hospital where she works as a

Amina (left) and Azra Kurtovic stand on the South Street Bridge in Philadelphia, Pennsylvania.

hematologist. Their father, Esad, had lost his chemical engineering job when the factory shut down.

Sadly, Amina and Azra lost family and friends to the shelling. "Our cousin died in the May 25 massacre in 1995," says Azra. "He was only eighteen."

"May 25 was celebrated as the day of youth for Yugoslavia and was also the birthday of Tito, the former president of Yugoslavia," recalls Amina. "That day, the enemy shelled the downtown area of the city, injuring around two hundred people and killing about seventy-one—most of them young."

"We saw our cousin only two days before he died," Azra states sadly.

"Yeah, I remember him talking about wanting to buy a motorcycle," adds Amina.

"And two of our school friends were wounded in the massacre—one of them lost her legs. She was transported to a neighboring country to recover, before returning home. So many people were wounded by the thousands of pieces of flying shells. Just a tiny piece can kill you," Azra describes. "Every time we heard something drop or heard a little sound, we automatically thought to ourselves, 'Run for cover.' In the beginning of the war, I was scared, but then I got used to it so it wasn't actually fear. One day, my friend and I were downtown, passing by a store, when we suddenly heard that

familiar whistling sound of a shell overhead. We just waited, knowing it would land somewhere nearby. It fell about ten meters away, and we ran into the nearest building. Luckily nobody was seriously injured."

After three turbulent years of the war, in June 1995, then fifteen-year-old Amina and Azra were sent to the United States on school scholarships—Amina to Friends Central School, just outside of Philadelphia, and Azra to Germantown Friends School in Philadelphia. Although the war ended at the close of that year, the sisters' parents felt they would still be safer going to school in the United States. They faced the challenge of living apart in a foreign country, with different host families and attending separate schools.

"That first year was hard," admits Amina. "We both felt that something was missing, even though we talked to each other every day. In Bosnia, we were always so close together."

"I think we were just missing each other because we were so used to being together all the time," says Azra.

Amina continues, "Our family and schools realized it would be much better for us to live together. So, the second year, I went to Azra's host family, the Sharpless family. We've been living together for the past two years, but we still go to different schools.

"The war made us appreciate the little things in life, like water and electricity—the things you don't usually pay attention to. Especially the first year, when we came right from the war. For example, when we'd go to the bathroom, we wouldn't turn the lights on because we forgot that there was electricity.

"We have a different perspective from our classmates. We can imagine worse situations than most people can imagine here," Amina says, admitting that she still has nightmares about the war. "We came here and would wonder why people were so concerned about certain things that didn't seem important to us. After a year we realized that's a normal reaction—in Bosnia we would do that if the war hadn't occurred."

"Being twins really helped us get through the war and gave us courage to travel to America," reflects Azra. "Whatever we face next, we know that there will always be somebody there for us."

"It's great to be twins—*blizankinjes,* as they call us in Bosnian. I have somebody to talk to, somebody who knows me, a best friend. If I have problems, Azra's always there and I'm always going to tell her. Even if I'm mad at her, I know

now that we've been going to different schools, we're developing more differences."

"I think we developed different characteristics when we came to the United States. We finally realized that, although we're twins, we are different. I think Amina's more serious, more conservative; and, I'm more optimistic and joyful. We sort of click together."

"So, even though people talk about us as one unit, since we've been apart more, we're kind of building the other half," Amina explains.

"I definitely think being separated a little was important," Azra agrees. "Otherwise we would

"Being twins really helped us get through the war.... Whatever we face next, we know that there will always be somebody there for us."

that she's always going to be there. And even though we're different, we often have the same thinking process. We like the same type of music, the same movies, and the same subjects in school. In Bosnia, if somebody asked us for an opinion, we would have . . ."

". . . exactly the same opinion," Azra laughs, finishing for her.

"For example, a conversation with her was almost like talking to myself—like 'Hi, Amina, how are you?' We'd observe things in the street the same way and comment on the same things. So I couldn't say, 'Look at that tree,' because I knew that Azra already looked at that tree and thought, 'Look at that tree.'"

"Sometimes, it was like talking to your conscience," smiles Azra.

"We thought so much alike," says Amina, "that we didn't have different opinions to share. But

never be able to figure out for ourselves who we really are."

Right now these high school seniors are on the verge of deciding their futures—determining whether they will attend different colleges in the United States or return to Bosnia to live together.

"Even if Amina and I separate, we're still going to be just as close. We'll probably call each other every day!"

Jim Lewis
Jim Springer

"It was kind of like standing there and looking at myself," says Jim Springer of the moment he met his twin—after thirty-nine years of being apart. "It wasn't like meeting a stranger. It felt great—like someone I hadn't seen for a long time." What's more, his brother, Jim Lewis, was given the same name by his adoptive parents.

So many questions went through Jim Springer's mind. "Why is he looking me up after all these years? Does he need a kidney? What kind of person is he? Will I like him?"

Authorities had told Jim Springer's parents, when they adopted him at six months of age, that his twin died at birth. But in his heart, Jim never really believed it.

Unlike Jim Springer, his twin brother, Jim Lewis, was told by his adoptive parents when he was six years old that he had a brother, possibly a twin. "A year after my adoption, when the judge asked my parents what they had named me, they said, 'James Edward.' Somebody in the courtroom spoke up and said, 'You can't name this boy James, because the other boy is named James.'"

But Jim Lewis didn't search for his brother for thirty-nine years—when he took a job with the local police department and learned how to do the search. "I can't tell you why I waited so long," he responds slowly. "I think it was God's will, because when it happened, it happened quickly. It just fell right into place.

"I was so nervous during our first meeting," he continues. "I mean, where do you start after thirty-nine years? Just where do you start?"

"It's not like going to see a baby sister in the hospital for the first time!" adds Jim Springer, the more outgoing of the two. "Other than different hair styles, we looked the same. Same weight, same height, our faces are the same. When we met, it was very emotional for awhile. We kind of stammered and stuttered. Finally, we got down to talking about our lives."

Jim Springer (left) and Jim Lewis spend time together at Jim Springer's vacation home on Fenner's Lake, Fort Loramie, Ohio.

That's when they found out they shared many uncanny similarities in their personal lives, aside from being named "Jim" by their adoptive parents. When they were young, living only forty-five minutes apart, they both grew up with adopted brothers named Larry. They both had a dog named Toy. One named his first son James Allen and the other named his son James Alan. And they both worked in similar jobs through the years—both serving as sheriff's deputies in nearby Ohio counties, law enforcement agents at the same time, and filling-station attendants.

"I don't know how we ever kept from running across one another!" exclaims fifty-eight-year-old Jim Lewis.

They both married first wives named Linda, divorced them and married second wives named Betty. "Of course, I'm married to a Sandy now," Jim Lewis adds, "and Jim gets a lot of ribbing over that."

"I'm not allowed to talk to any women named Sandy!" his twin laughs.

And the extraordinary parallels continued. They smoked the same brand of cigarettes, drank the same brand of beer, had a nervous habit of nail-biting, and enjoyed math and disliked spelling in school. They used the same slang words. Neither enjoyed sports but instead practiced woodworking. Both built a white bench around a tree in their respective yards. "We found out that we had even vacationed in the same spot on the Florida coast," Jim Springer adds, "at about the same time of year." That is—after driving their Chevrolets to get there.

Dr. Thomas J. Bouchard of the University of Minnesota read about their 1979 reunion and contacted them immediately, asking them to participate in the Minnesota Study of Twins Reared Apart. The study addresses questions surrounding the nature (genes) versus nurture (environment) debate. Identical twins separated at birth and reunited later in life are perfect subjects for such a study. These twin pairs, whose numbers are decreasing because of changes in adoption laws, share the same genes but, having been raised in different environments, allow researchers to better isolate the effect of genes on human development. The brothers agreed to participate, and were aptly named "the Jim Twins."

The Minnesota Twin Study entailed a wide variety of tests.

"You name it, we did it," Jim Springer quips.

In fact, they had to do it more than once.

"We were so close on the tests that we had to do them over again because Dr. Bouchard was afraid that if we didn't, nobody was going to believe the results. They would think we copied off each other, even though we were isolated in separate booths!" Jim Lewis chuckles. So, one full week of tests and 20,000 questions later, Dr. Bouchard's team was still astonished.

The Jim Twins displayed similar voice tones, body language, and gestures, and had very similar scores on personality, intelligence, and aptitude tests. Even their medical histories were nearly identical—both had high blood pressure, similar pulse rates, vasectomies, suffered from tension/migraine headaches that began at age eighteen, had "lazy eye" in the same eye, and both had experienced what they thought were heart attacks. The majority of traits—personality as well as physical—assessed by the Minnesota Twin Study show a significant genetic influence, although researchers recognize that the environment also influences the expression of these traits.

The first year after their reunion, they participated in a whirlwind of interviews, television shows, more twin studies, and travels throughout the world. "We didn't have to worry about plans to be together—other people made plans for us," Jim Springer smiles thankfully. "They would have two rooms waiting for us. We'd tell them, 'We don't need two rooms, just

Their experience has been so powerful that Jim Lewis and Jim Springer have helped other twins find their twin. "I hope our story helps someone—maybe encourages them to look up someone; or if they've already found that person, to make it good for themselves," Jim Lewis says.

"I certainly hope so," adds his brother, "because there's nothing but good for us!"

So good, that they've made several promises to one another. "We promised that nobody would ever come between us, that we would always try to spend as much time as possible with one another, and that we'd never lose one another again. We agreed that we'd always be truthful with each other," says Jim Springer.

Sadly, Jim Lewis admits, "There were some twins who got together and it didn't work out. Their personalities just clashed. It hurts me to see twins

"We promised that nobody would ever come between us, that we would always try to spend as much time as possible with another, and that we'd never lose one another again."

one with two beds.' We do television shows—we have fun and come home. That's it. The satisfaction is, I found my brother."

"If I have a problem in life, big or small, I can go to Jim," adds Jim Springer. "We've never had to work at our relationship. It comes naturally."

Today, Jim and Jim live eighty-five miles apart and don't get to spend as much time together as they'd like. They see each other only once every few months as both are busy with families and jobs.

"If we lived closer to one another, you can bet your boots we'd be together more," Jim Lewis, now a school custodian, states confidently. He writes his brother almost daily, while Jim Springer, working long hours as a substation electrician, responds every chance he gets. Neither has e-mail. "Thank God," says Jim Lewis, "because we'd burn the lights out, I think!"

get into arguments. Then they won't see each other. Some day they're really going to regret that."

It's hard to imagine how their lives would be if the Jim Twins had never met. "We try not to think about that," says Jim Lewis.

"Yeah, that would be a very sad thought," Jim Springer adds. "Thirty-nine years was bad enough."

"What's sad about it is, Jim and I were never raised together," says Jim Lewis, "and we never experienced a lot of things that brothers do . . . playing together and things like that. We can't make up for lost time, but we're going to try."

Jacqueline Hennessy
Jill Hennessy

When Canadian actress Jill Hennessy landed a role as a twin call girl in the 1988 motion picture *Dead Ringers,* she didn't need a body double. Instead, her identical twin, Jacqueline, played the part perfectly.

In film and in real life, however, being twins is a role the twenty-eight-year-old Hennessys take seriously. "We're strong opponents of twinsploitation," declares Jacqueline.

Which, Jill explains, is "the dehumanizing portrayal of twins on TV or in film in which they are rendered into this single entity that isn't whole unless the two are together. Twins are individuals who don't always have to be dressed alike or stand together to feel special or whole."

Known as "Jacq and Jill," the Hennessys epitomize this balance between closeness and individuality. Although they share the same creative propensity, they have chosen different means of expression. Jacq, who earned a master's degree in French literature, currently works as an editorial contributor to the Canadian women's magazine *Chatelaine*. In her free time, she writes short stories, takes photographs, and paints. Jill, an actress perhaps best known for her three-year role as no-nonsense Assistant District Attorney Claire Kincaid on *Law and Order*, has since let her hair down and returned to films, including the action thriller *Most Wanted*, the romantic comedy *A Smile Like Yours*, and her recent works *Dead Broke* and *Chutney Popcorn*.

"Jill and I have diverse interests that we individually want to explore," says Jacq. "And by no means are our careers going to remain fixed. Our interests are always diverging, overlapping and evolving."

"Being twins," Jill points out, "we get to explore two different lives and live vicariously

Jill (left) and Jacq Hennessy hang out at a Greenwich Village coffee shop in New York City.

through each other. I get to see Jacq pursue something that I would have liked to do."

"And vice versa. We kind of jump roles all the time," Jacq explains. "I'll go on the set with Jill, and she'll read my work or attend classes with me. Jill does everything that I do. She speaks French, and she writes and paints. She also speaks Italian and Spanish."

"I don't really consider Jacq's profession much different than mine," Jill affirms. "I know that she's a great actress. And I've never divided us into categories like, 'Oh she's the writer, and I'm the actress.' I perceive her as a writer, actress, and painter—basically most of the things that I'm interested in, as well."

"Don't forget our singing, Jill!"

"We sing together, and I play guitar. We do the Indigo Girls—we cover anything, babe!"

"That's our ultimate dream, although we'll never claim to be as good as the Indigo Girls," Jacq laughs. "We'd love to work together. While Jill's acting and I'm writing, we'd like to put together our own band, a duo, and put out an album."

At age seventeen, Jacq and Jill decided to pursue different dreams. "The detour point was when I decided not to go to grade thirteen and Jacq did. In Canada, grade thirteen is a preparatory year for college. I moved to Toronto, which was tough because part of me really wanted to stay with Jacq and pursue a

scholastic route. But the other part of me just had to try acting. I knew I'd regret it if I didn't at least try."

"The funny thing is, Jill always did really well in school," recalls Jacq. "She won all kinds of awards—best music student, best this, best that. And I hated school—I didn't do homework, I was a total bum. It's ironic that I'm the one who went on for a master's degree."

"One of my acting teachers who was a twin once told me that twins have a double separation—not only do they have to separate emotionally from their parents at some point, but they have to separate from their twin," Jill recalls. "We were around thirteen when there was some conflict at home. Jacq and I dealt with it in different ways. During those years, I don't remember being with her that much. An outsider looking at that situation might say, 'Gee, why didn't they get closer together?' I'm still trying to figure that one out, but what's funny is that we've gotten closer afterward. Maybe we needed to separate and then come back together again."

"It was a very weird time," reflects Jacq. "Our parents had just separated. Jill's way of avoiding the whole family situation was by diving into her schoolwork, staying home, baking and reading. Whereas I avoided it by not being home, hanging out with friends instead. I still feel guilty to this day for leaving Jill alone at home."

"Oh Jacq, I don't want you to feel guilty," says Jill.

•   •   •

"The only competition we feel is competition that people force upon us," Jacq states. "A lot of people were disappointed if we dressed differently. They thought we weren't entertaining them enough."

"And it's so frustrating when other people try to compartmentalize us," Jill adds. "Especially being in an industry where my picture is displayed in different places, and I'm often dressed in designer gowns with special makeup and hairstyles. People love to comment on both of us, and ask, 'Who's the fat one? Who's the smart one? Who's meaner?'"

Jacq interrupts sarcastically, "I am! I'm the stupid one—like anyone's really going to answer that question and not be humiliated. Yet I can't really blame people," she admits, "because being a twin is such a different concept. I know a lot of people would love to have a twin, so I try to be understanding, even though sometimes it does hurt in a way. I try to illustrate the point that we're two individuals. I'm not sure if I've ever said this to anybody, but sometimes I'd like to say, 'How would you feel if I took you and your best friend and systematically compared (1) your body shapes and (2) which one was smarter?' Inevitably, that

compare themselves with their own siblings," she winks. "I came out three minutes earlier and was skinny as a rake. Jill was nice and plump. That woman was monopolizing all the food in the womb. On top of it, she was crowding me—I just had to get out. And I'm sure she was trying to stuff me back in and get out herself."

Amid the jokes and candor, Jacq and Jill's unwavering support for each other shines through. Jill is the first to read her sister's short stories and rave about Jacq's talents and successes. And when asked which movie was her best, Jill trusts Jacq's judgment best. "My first instinct is to ask my sister. Jacq, what's the best movie I've done?"

Jacq enthusiastically replies, "It depends—so many of the episodes of *Law and Order* were my

"I came out three minutes earlier and was skinny as a rake. Jill was nice and plump. That woman was monopolizing all the food in the womb."

person would find the experience very dehumanizing and degrading. And that's what it feels like for twins when they're compared. We're not freaks, we're not the exact same person. Genetically we carry the same code, and there's a very unique bond; however, we still have very separate experiences and are very different individuals.

"The funniest and most outrageous thing to me, which I can't comprehend, is why the first question that everybody asks a twin is, 'Who's older?'" Jacq smiles. "Oh, you mean which one hit the air first? Who emerged from the womb first? But I guess it's understandable because that's the only way poor single-birth people

favorites. And her recent movie *Chutney Popcorn* was one of the best films I've seen her in. She was just fantastic. She was so real, so believable. You could really sympathize with her character."

"I'm glad she likes it," smiles Jill. "I love this movie. I play the girlfriend of a woman who's of Indian descent, and her family disapproves of our relationship."

Jacq adds candidly, "I must admit, as a twin, it throws you for a loop if your twin's straight and

you see her in a lesbian love scene with this woman—even though it wasn't a hot and heavy love scene or anything. It was just a romantic cut."

"I sort of felt uncomfortable for my sister," concedes Jill. "While I was watching this love scene I was thinking, 'Boy, it must be weird for my twin, watching me, who looks like her, on screen doing a love scene.' Regardless of whether it's with another woman or a man, it's a very weird thing. Because it's an intimate moment, and you're watching somebody who you have a huge connection with—plus, they look a lot like you. It's almost like seeing yourself in that role."

"Actually you're right," Jacq agrees. "It's so funny—I can't watch her love scenes. When she's kissing guys I don't know, I can't watch. I cringe because it's far too intimate. They're strangers to me."

"I think it's such a unique human experience to have somebody who is your soul mate," muses Jill. "It's the closest equivalent you can have to somebody walking the earth who you know will always be there for you and understand you. The twin relationship is a microcosm of the whole human experience of intimacy. As twins, you develop a high level of intimacy at a very young age. And I think all of society is trying to deal with being intimate in so many different ways."

Jacq chimes in. "It evokes a lot of feelings in people—feelings of discomfort because intimacy is something they might either fear or desire. If you're in a healthy twin relationship—if you've been brought up in a family that nurtures your bond as well as your individuality—you can pass that experience on to your other relationships, inevitably making that bond with your partner or spouse even better. I've had such a close bond with Jill all my life that it's something I can carry on, something I'm good at now. I think it's easier for me to be comfortable in an intimate relationship. Sometimes people who normally find intimate relationships difficult are at ease around me. I don't know if it's a vibe twins give off, or what. Maybe it's my deodorant," she laughs.

"I think it depends on how healthily that twin relationship is nurtured by the parents," Jill says. "And I think there needs to be a textbook laid out for parents of twins—particularly parents who are single-birth people who may not understand the twin bond, which can be the greatest gift to a child. We would like to thank our parents because they didn't tell us that our self-worth centered around our being twins—we weren't nurtured solely as a unit. But if children were not seen as special unless they were within a unit, then the twin relationship might compete with other intimate relationships, causing problems. Another thing about being a twin—I remember learning the word 'equality' at a very young age. There's a desire not to get the short end of the stick, but also of not wanting to come out on top either—not wanting to hurt the other one by getting something she doesn't have. You start to develop empathy a little earlier. Not that you treat your twin with the greatest respect all the time," Jill admits.

"That's for sure!" quips Jacq with a grin.

Raymond Brandt
Robert Brandt

On July 5, 1949, twenty-year-old identical twins Raymond and Robert Brandt were working as electrical linesmen atop separate utility poles about five miles apart. "All of a sudden," says Raymond, "I experienced this tremendous electrical jolt in my body, and I was mystified because I wasn't working energized conductors—but my twin was. And I felt . . . I felt Robert's spirit separate from mine. I said, 'Take me with you . . . take me with you. . . .'

"My supervisor told me to come down, but I already knew what he was going to say. I knew it the very moment it happened. 'You don't have to tell me,' I told him. 'My twin's dead. I felt his shock.'"

Raymond has recounted the tragic event on some twenty-three national TV shows. Each time, the tears, emotions, and sense of loss are just as raw and powerful. "It's always as if it just happened yesterday. It's as if half of you has died,

yet your twin continues on in a spiritual realm," he says, his voice heavy.

For many twinless twins, these feelings often transform into deep depression and thoughts of suicide while yearning to be with their "other half." Considering how much he shared with his brother, Raymond struggled for years to accept his loss.

"We were numbers three and four of eleven kids," explains Raymond. "We grew up in the small German-American farming community of Ridgeville Corners, Ohio, where we were well-known as the 'Brandt Twins' or, in German, *zweillings*. We were inseparable. We were in complete union. If one of us got spanked, we had the other one for comfort. We always took the blame for each other and worked as a team."

This teamwork came naturally for the Brandt twins, as they had plenty of company: identical twin nephews, two sets of identical twin uncles on their mother's side, and two sets of identical

Raymond Brandt walks on St. Joe
Road near his home in Fort Wayne, Indiana.

85

twin cousins. Their paternal grandmother, an identical twin herself, had stillborn identical twins. Raymond's sister has the only set of fraternal twins in the family.

With so many Brandt twins, there was confusion at times. "Our mom came in from the farm to prepare lunch one day," recalls Raymond with a smile. "She had put a ribbon in the hair of one of us to tell us apart, and the ribbon was on the floor. She didn't know which one it belonged to, so she just pinned it on. I may have been baptized 'Robert'—it doesn't really matter. I am Robert and Robert is me."

"My twin and I were reared in austere conditions," Raymond continues. "Our family was poor, and yet we never knew we were poor because we had God's greatest gift—we had each other. That's all we needed."

They were planning to go to college together, Robert to be a Lutheran pastor working with children, Raymond to be a pediatrician. "My twin went to college alone one semester because it was easier to get churches to fund his schooling," explains Raymond. "But we couldn't stand to be apart. So he dropped out and we agreed that we'd work for a couple of years, make a little nest egg, and then we'd go back to college together." That's when Raymond and Robert began working as electrical linesmen.

It took half a lifetime of intense suffering before Raymond could accept Robert's death. "The first five years were a total blackout," he recalls. He dismisses the medals of valor he earned in the Korean War soon after his twin's death. "What they thought was heroism was simply recklessness and a lack of fear of death. Nobody could understand the severity of my pain. I didn't know any other twinless twins. For thirty-five years I even felt that I was no longer a twin."

The turning point came when a pastor advised Raymond to write a letter to Robert, expressing things left unsaid and his sorrow for blocking his twin out of his life. In writing the letter, Raymond also found a message for himself. "That's when I decided to dedicate my life to helping other twinless twins."

After attending his first International Twin Association Convention in 1984, in Fort Wayne, Raymond was struck by the fact that there was no representative for twinless twins. Yet it is inevitable that half of a twinship will feel this terrible loss at some point in life. He founded the Twinless Twin Support Group International in 1986 and serves as director of the 1,700-member organization, with the tireless support of his wife, Miriam, his "right arm" for the last nine years.

In addition to his organization work, Raymond publishes the quarterly *Twinsworld Magazine* for twins and all multiple-birth people as well as *Twinless Times*, which is specifically for the Twinless Twin Support Group. He receives thousands of letters and phone calls, organizes twinless twin conventions and meetings nationwide, and has had a child care and education center, LAMB Ministries, dedicated in honor of his twin. Even his own battle with cancer—diagnosed in 1995—has not slowed Raymond's efforts. When asked what gives him the endless energy and inspiration, he simply answers, "Robert."

To the thousands of twinless sufferers who contact him, Raymond offers the same advice that saved him years before: "The first step," he says, "is recognizing that you are still a twin. It took me thirty-five years to find the first twin who said to me, 'Well, my God, if you're born a twin, you die a twin.' And I think that whatever your faith, most twinless twins derive ultimate strength from a belief that life continues in some form beyond death."

He continues, "The single greatest therapy for twinless twins is to turn their attention to another twin. And that's what we teach at these conferences—the H-H Twins. You Heal by Helping others.

"You're not jealous of twins who have their understand but they can only start learning what it is to be a twin. You're not saying twins are better or twins are worse or twins are odd or twins are strange. Twins are very different, especially in this grieving phenomenon.

"And twins can never know what it is to be a single-birth person because, from Day One, twins have been two. They have what we've identified now as this in-utero bonding phenomenon." With ultrasound and sonograms, scientists have even documented such activity as hand-holding, kissing, and hugging between twins in the womb.

"With a twinless twin, it's as if one of you suddenly evaporated, throwing you into a chasm of constantly looking and seeking," Raymond explains. As an example, he points out the drive of a famous twinless twin—Elvis Presley, whose twin, Jesse, died at birth. "Elvis referred to his twin as his original bodyguard and spiritual guide through life.

"More people than we realize were conceived as twins, but one of the twins had an absorption. This is known as the vanishing twin phenomenon,

"I've now had forty-seven years of separateness from him—I would not trade those twenty years for those forty-seven. Never. One moment of twinship is worth a lifetime."

twin; you are thankful for them because you relish their totalness. I've also found that twins have an innate sense for other twins, like there's a genetic magnet."

Raymond's positive energy attracts twins and non-twins alike, which is critical in helping others deal with a twin's loss.

"Bridging the gap between the multiple-birth world and the single-birth world is one of the biggest necessary hurdles. First of all, single-birth people have to rinse their mind of any previous concepts they have about twins. Invite your readers to have a mindset that allows for the believability of twins being different and to try not to fit them into a single-birth model or mold.

"They have to accept that they will never and its effect on the surviving twin cannot be ignored," Raymond adds.

At age sixty-eight, Raymond has earned two doctorates in human engineering. Yet his accomplishments mean surprisingly little compared to his twinship. "Even though we had only twenty years together physically—and I've now had forty-seven years of separateness from him—I would not trade those twenty years for those forty-seven. Never. One moment of twinship is worth a lifetime."

Jeff Wang
Julie Wang

"It's fun to see people's reactions when they find out we're brother and sister, let alone twins. Usually they're really surprised because we look nothing alike," says nineteen-year-old Julie Wang about her fraternal twin brother, Jeff. "Jeff is significantly taller than I am—he's five foot, nine inches tall, and I'm five feet tall."

Jeff and Julie Wang are freshmen at Duke University in North Carolina.

"We feel lucky to be boy-girl twins rather than identical or same-sex twins," says Jeff candidly, "because it's not like looking in a mirror and constantly being compared."

"There's less competition—with friends, academics, and athletics," Julie finishes. "I know some identical twin girls who are very cut-throat with each other simply because they're always compared. But in our case, there are different standards for boys and girls."

Jeff describes other differences between them. "I enjoy art and play the guitar, and she's happy with her engineering and science." In high school, Jeff played football, basketball, and volleyball, while Julie enjoyed tennis, badminton, and soccer and served on the cheerleading squad.

"Julie's always been more mature," Jeff continues, pointing out how he likes to tease his sister while she watches TV, "by dancing and putting my hands really close to her face without touching her. She'll just walk away or yell at me. I think it's a boy-girl thing—girls mature faster than boys. Even in second grade when we would argue, Julie would sarcastically say, 'Oh, Jeff, you're right. You are one hundred percent correct.' She would just say that to end the argument. But that would get the worst rise out of me!"

Despite their differences, the two have not

Jeff and Julie Wang sit on the High Street beach on Lake Michigan in Chicago.

been immune to comparisons, especially in junior high school, when they shared many classes. "Some of our teachers would lump us into one person and say, 'Oh, the Wangs had the highest score.' It was assumed that if Julie did well on a test, I'd have to do well on a test."

Jeff and Julie have similar academic goals, but are pursuing different interests. Julie is currently majoring in biomedical engineering with a pre-med focus, while Jeff is studying economics, with a minor in Japanese, and taking science classes to fulfill pre-med requirements. They remain close friends, living two dorms apart and seeing each other almost daily.

Julie remembers times when she and her brother were not close. When

"My mother has always emphasized that no matter what, we always have each other."

"As we've grown up, I accept more punches from her without punching her back," Jeff teases, "because I'd crush her now!" He adds more seriously, "I realize that as long as I live, there will always be someone who started at the same exact time and the same exact place. I feel that I will always have a friend who's living a parallel life to mine, even though she's a girl and I'm a guy. She's my sister, but I sometimes treat her like a brother. I'm not embarrassed by some of the things I say in front of her—about dating, for example."

"The big thing about being twins is that we're

"We feel lucky to have an unconditional, lifelong friend. My mother has always emphasized that no matter what, we always have each other."

they were six months old, she and Jeff traveled to Taiwan; Julie remained there for a few years while Jeff returned home with their mother. "I stayed with my dad while he finished school. When we returned to America, I didn't recognize my mom and my brother as family, so I treated them like guests or strangers for a while."

"I remember thinking Julie was terribly spoiled because my relatives in Taiwan gave her so much attention, and she had bags full of toys."

"I didn't let Jeff play with the toys, either!" Julie admits.

"When she got back, I used to bite her—I think I was jealous because I had to share the attention with her."

Their fighting lasted until junior high school. "We used to throw notebooks and pens at each other," recalls Julie. "I don't know how my mom coped with it."

But with maturity has come a deeper appreciation of their relationship—they now support each other and value each other's advice.

"We feel lucky to have an unconditional, lifelong friend," Julie explains.

peers—the same age group," Julie adds. "It's not like he's older and therefore I have to listen to him, or I'm older and he has to do what I say. But it works both ways."

"Except when we're driving in the car with my mom, I always get the front seat," Jeff teases.

"You're right, Jeff. I don't know how that happened!"

Nautica Sereno
Quincy Sereno

Seventeen-year-old Drisana Sereno remembers worrying about leaving one of her newborn sons at the hospital. She had thought, "I can't leave him here. I'm supposed to protect him. Will he be all right? Will he know that I'm gone? Will he miss his brother?" She hated leaving Nautica behind when she and Quincy went home.

Born four weeks early at four pounds, five ounces, Nautica was seven ounces lighter than his identical twin brother, Quincy. "Sometimes in the womb, one twin receives less nutrients than the other, and may need special monitoring," Drisana explains. "Nautica did throughout my pregnancy."

• • •

Three and a half years have passed since those tense weeks of waiting and wondering. Quincy and Nautica rush to their mother to share a kiss. Both are healthy and full of vigor—their energetic play disguises any hint of Nautica's earlier struggle in life. They take turns bouncing off the sofa, their socks barely hanging onto their feet, then perform somersaults and proudly finish with a bow.

Drisana recalls feeling scared and lonely in her new role as a single, teenage mother of twins. She had been living in New York City, far from her family in California. Quincy and Nautica's father was not involved in their lives, and her parents had strongly disapproved of her pregnancy. Drisana found herself in a downward spiral after the twins were born. At one point, she and her baby sons lived in a homeless shelter for a few weeks. All the while she feared that, without a permanent home, her children might be taken from her.

When Drisana's father visited his grandchildren, "he realized that I was still his daughter," Drisana recounts, "and that he loved me and my children." He invited her to move

Quincy (left) and Nautica Sereno play on the beach in La Jolla, California, near their home.

back home with her sons. Drisana is now pursuing a college degree. Her parents are supportive and have become strongly attached to Quincy and Nautica. "We are a very affectionate family—we're always hugging and kissing," Drisana says.

· · ·

Quincy and Nautica obviously enjoy each other as they race around from the swings to the slide set and finally to their toy Batmobile, which they take turns crashing off the side of an armchair. "They learned to say 'It's my turn now'

they push one another to reach their next developmental stage. "One learned to sit, the other learned to sit. One learned to roll, the other learned to roll really quickly—almost always within a week of each other. It goes back and forth."

While Quincy and Nautica are the lights of their mother's life, Drisana notes that raising twins has not been easy. "At night, they want me to simultaneously tuck them into bed, but I can't be at both places at once! And they fight a lot right now, usually about sharing toys and attention."

Quincy and Nautica suddenly run outside and jump into their identical yellow and red race cars. They crouch down in their seats and, on some unspoken cue, pedal their cars into each other with a crash and a squeal.

"They are not the same little boys—they are totally different," asserts Drisana. "For example, Nautica's really physical and kinesthetic, and has a lot of energy. He likes to play rough. He bonds well with women, maybe because of all of the nurses who took care of him in the hospital. Quincy, on the other hand, is more auditory—he likes to talk and listen. He's very imaginative and sensitive to peoples' emotions. He loves to give hugs." She

"They learned to say, 'It's my turn now' about a year ago. . . . Nautica, who's the second-born, once asked me, 'Mommy, when can I be first born?'"

about a year ago. Everybody is really impressed with that," says Drisana. "In fact, Nautica, who's the second-born, once asked me, 'Mommy, when can I be first-born?'

"When they were infants," she continues, "they used to stare at one another and crack up laughing. And they like to fool people. For example, people will ask Nautica, 'Are you Quincy?' And Nautica will say, 'Yeah,' and then Quincy will say, 'Yeah, and I'm Nautica.' They do that all the time." Drisana smiles at her sons' antics.

Quincy and Nautica are a good team. They take turns pushing each other on the rope swing in the backyard, perhaps the same way

speculates that her sons have developed such distinct personalities due to their different experiences in the womb or shortly after birth.

Quincy and Nautica's relationship is a balance between their individuality and their closeness. "I don't try to push them together or apart," Drisana explains. "They're brothers, and they love each other, but they also need to be themselves."

To prove her point, Drisana asks her son, "Are you a twin, Nautica?" To which he emphatically responds, "I'm Nautica!" He throws his hand in the air for emphasis, then runs over to give Quincy a hug. The balance is struck.

Betsy McCagg
Mary McCagg

The McCaggs' bodies slid forward in unison. Then their arms pulled as their legs pushed backward in a burst of power and grace. These twin rowers appeared like dual images of each other—strong figures bending and leaning in tandem—like two fine-tuned pistons propelling their two-person boat forward.

one ... two ... one ... two ...

Mary maintained the rhythmic count from behind. The boat's smooth path through the water belied the sheer, raw power on board.

Later, 6'2" Mary and Betsy McCagg, known as the "Twin Towers," stood side-by-side on the podium of the 1995 Pan-American Games to accept their gold medals in rowing for the 2,000-meter pair race.

This race was particularly meaningful for them—it was the first gold medal that the McCaggs won in a major international race in a two-person boat.

"When we crossed the finish line, we knew that whatever the outcome, we had achieved something special involving just the two of us," recalls Mary. "To hear that we had won was icing on the cake."

Racing and training in the pair requires an extreme amount of dedication and focus. "Betsy and I really like the pair race. I love the fact that my sister and I are able to fulfill our dreams of athletic achievement together. When we're in our pair, there's nowhere to hide. We have only each other to rely on for strength and encouragement, and also for blame."

"When an eight-person boat wins a medal," explains Betsy, "there's a great sense of team camaraderie. Twenty-seven people—nine per boat—are on the winner's podium, but in a two-person race, there are only six people up there—two per boat—so we stand out more.

Betsy (left) and Mary McCagg row in their pair on the Charles River in Boston, Massachusetts.

When we took off our hats on the podium, there was a moment when everybody realized, 'Oh, they're twins!' "

•   •   •

Betsy and Mary's accomplishment had taken years of intense training and determination—the same dedication that helped them win multiple World Championship Rowing events in two- and eight-person boats. Their team, the U.S. National Team, won silver medals in 1993 and 1994, and gold medals in 1995.

The McCaggs' successes also include competing in the eight-person race in the 1992 Olympic Games in in Barcelona, Spain, where they came in sixth place. In 1996, in the Atlanta, Georgia, games, they placed fourth closely behind Romania, Belarussia, and Canada. Now they have returned their focus to the two-person race as they approach the next Olympic Games. Mary is on the Athlete Advisory Council for the U.S. Olympic Committee and the Board of U.S. Rowing, while Betsy is on the Board of the National Rowing Foundation.

•   •   •

Twenty-nine-year-old Betsy and Mary describe their twinship as a huge blessing that provides them with the strength to reach their highest goals. But they have also experienced the down side of their relationship when they were forced to row on different teams—and sometimes even to compete against one another.

"In 1994, Betsy and I were in the final stages of selection for the World Championship Rowing Team," Mary says. "Our coach felt we needed to change the line-up, and that change was me. Betsy would remain in the eight-person boat, and I could try to race for a spot on the team with a new partner at the pair trials in a week."

Betsy offered to sacrifice her position in the eight and try out with Mary in the pair, but Mary resisted. "How could I allow the chance that neither of us would make the team when she had already secured a spot?" To their surprise, their coaches and teammates could not comprehend their quandary.

"To them there was no question of what to do," says Mary with disbelief. "Betsy should remain with them. They didn't view this as a choice between my team or my sister, but as a simple issue of following coach's orders.

"I don't think we've ever spent a more torturous twenty-four hours," Mary admits. "But in the end, I left for pair trials with my new partner of one day, leaving Betsy frustrated from the no-win situation." Mary won the trial and was able to compete at the Worlds, but for the first time Betsy was not her roommate. "She came away with a silver medal and I placed sixth," adds Mary. "I was glad to have made it to the finals, and was both jealous of and happy for Betsy."

"Having a twin is both a godsend and a curse," Betsy admits. "While it definitely brought us notoriety as a unit, it also implied that we weren't as significant on the singular level. People say, 'Oh, the twins are here,' and we respond, 'We're two people, there are two of us! Do any of you even know what our real names are, or do you just know us as *the twins?*'"

There was another down side to being twins—the constant comparisons.

"Betsy routinely beat me on tests on the rowing machines and ergometers. Our coach would yell, 'Come on, you're twins! Why don't you row like twins? Yet, whenever the scrutiny was almost too much to bear," adds Mary, "I knew I always had my sister fighting alongside me and rooting for me when I had to test alone." Their relationship, as with any close bond, is filled with intense emotions—feelings these Harvard graduates are not afraid to express.

"We're brutally honest with each other," Betsy smiles.

"On the water we're known almost as much for our fighting as for our speed," laughs Mary. "However, we prefer to label them 'verbal exchanges at high volume.'"

"We are always sisters and friends once practice is over," Betsy says.

Just as intense as their "verbal exchanges" are their non-verbal ones. Their teammates have, in

"I think it's hard for one person, let alone both of us, to make it into the realm of elite athletics," asserts Betsy.

"We had three or four practices a day, usually six and often seven days a week, for virtually all of the three years preceding the Games in Atlanta. I know with utter certainty," Mary states, "that I would not have survived if I hadn't had my sister to complain to, laugh with, cry to, and commiserate with in our mutual states of exhaustion."

Mary and Betsy also live together in Boston, Massachusetts, and work in the same retail bank merchandising company during the off-season. "What's the big deal?" Mary asks. "It's not

"I would not have survived if I hadn't had my sister to complain to, laugh with, cry to, and commiserate with...."

fact, chastised Mary and Betsy for their habit of standing close together, looking at each other, and seemingly communicating without words.

"I don't know if we can do this just because we've been with each other so much, or if there's actually some unique 'twin speak' occurring," Mary says, "but it has done a good job of perpetuating the twin myth on our team."

The attention their twinship generates has also caused tension among fellow rowers.

"During the Olympics," Betsy explains, "journalists wanted to interview us because we were twins in the same boat. Acquaintances would ask, 'Why are you special—just because there are two of you?'" The McCagg sisters do not seek out this attention, though they recognize why it happens.

weird—it's like living with your best friend. Why wouldn't I want to live with her?"

Whether or not they continue to live and row together, one thing is clear—the McCaggs are deeply devoted to each other.

"Maybe we'll retire with these fantastic memories of Argentina in the spring, the winter in Australia, and the summers in Prague or Switzerland or Finland," Mary muses.

"Or maybe," Betsy says, "we'll make one final stand in the 2000 Games in Sydney, Australia, in the pairs—just the two of us against the world."

Kelley Tesfaye
Maze Tesfaye

Ethiopian identical twins Kelley and Maze Tesfaye have filled their cozy family establishment, Twins Lounge, with a grand piano, colorful African prints, and authentic Ethiopian food.

Forty-three-year-old Kelley and Maze are no strangers to the warmth of a close family. Aside from being separated for one tumultuous year—when Kelley first traveled to the United States—they have lived together all their lives.

"We're very close. We care about and protect each other," Kelley explains. "We help each other—money-wise, knowledge-wise. We share everything. My big sister used to live with us, and she would say, 'If I tell you a secret, you're going to tell Maze!'"

Born in a country that holds one of the highest twin birth rates in the world, Kelley and Maze are familiar with diverse African twin mythology—ranging from twins being seen as a village curse for which they were ostracized or killed, to twins being revered as "familiars of the gods." Maze recalls her personal experience with an Ethiopian myth about twins.

"There's a superstition that fraternal boy-girl twins should not grow up together. After they are raised separately to a certain age, the twins are brought together. Like our fraternal twin boy-girl cousins—one stayed with their mother, the other with their aunt, until they were grown.

"I also hear that if one twin dies, the other will never stay too long. Maybe if they are too attached to one another, the other one will worry too much—just like husbands and wives who've been married for so many years."

Unfortunately, their closeness was not compatible with their marital relationships. Kelley and Maze are both separated from men they met and married in America.

"Our husbands got jealous because Kelley and I care so much about each other," Maze explains.

"My husband was always telling me, 'Why

Kelley (left) and Maze Tesfaye oversee their restaurant and jazz club, Twins Lounge, in Washington, D.C.

don't you marry your sister?'" Kelley adds. "But my relationship with Maze and my relationship with him were not the same. They were different."

The sisters are proud of their family. Both have two children—Maze has a son, Michael, and a daughter, Natalie, while Kelley has two daughters, Layla and Love-leigh, who have all been raised together. "We live in the same house and eat at the same table," Kelley says. "The children call me Mommy and they call Maze Mommy, also." The sisters' eighty-four-year-old mother, Belayensh, who still cooks some of her own recipes in the Twins Lounge kitchen, also lives with them. It is this sense of familial closeness—a mixture of their cultural background and their twinship—that the Tesfaye twins generously share with all who enter their Washington, D.C., club, every night from 9:30 P.M. to 2:00 A.M.

"'We feel at home, like we're in our dining room,' customers and musicians tell us. They can come into the kitchen to taste the food anytime. It's real casual," Kelley says.

"We play old jazz here, not the contemporary jazz you hear on the radio," Maze declares. The restaurant has featured greats such as Shirley Horn, Barry Harris, Randy Weston, Harold Mabern, Gil Scott Heron, and Gary Bartz.

"The famous musicians come here not for the money," Kelley acknowledges. "We cannot afford to pay them much. But they like the place. They like the food. It's funny—sometimes almost everybody in the audience is a musician!"

The success of the Twins Lounge is the culmination of teamwork through years of struggle and hard work beginning when the sisters left their homeland.

"When I left Ethiopia I was eighteen years old," Maze remembers. "Kelley came first, in 1971, and I came in 1972. The people were trying to overthrow King Haile Selassie, 'The Lion of Judah,' so my father sent us to America to finish college on a student visa." But the money for school never arrived. "As soon as we came, they overthrew the king. The money for our schooling stopped immediately.

"We worked hard as maids, waitresses, cashiers, hostesses, and bartenders," continues Maze. "We went to school in the daytime and worked at night. Kelley graduated in business management. I graduated in biology, then I went back to school to study nursing."

After years of working for other people, they had a revelation. "Instead of spending money to get advanced degrees, we said, 'Let's run a business together.' I found this restaurant in the newspaper," Maze says. "It's so small that we knew we could handle it. Because we value our relationship so much, we decided to name the club 'Twins Lounge.' We used the money that we had saved—$30,000—with some help from our brother," explains Maze.

It's been more than ten years since the opening day of their club, and Twins Lounge is still running smoothly. "Kelley runs the club full-time. I work as a registered nurse at Howard University Hospital, but I also work at Twins on my days off," says Maze.

"One time we decided to have a twins night, which was very successful," Kelley remembers. "Along with many twin customers, the bass player and drummer were twins, the piano player and saxophone player were twins, and the vocalists were twins. People say twins are always good luck. That's what I know so far! I think we're good luck."

Ralph Mendez
Robert Mendez

Robert and Ralph Mendez are part of a team of highly respected Los Angeles physicians at the forefront of kidney transplantation. "When we operate together, it's sort of automatic. We can go through a whole surgery and not say a word," describes Ralph. "It's just like four hands out of the same brain. We can operate in about half the time of somebody else."

"There is a lot of synergy working together," says Robert, "and many benefits from being twins, especially in the service field, where you have to interact with other people. Patients see the same familiar face and feel very comfortable. When I'm off-duty and he's taking calls for me, it appears as if the same person's taking calls twenty-four hours a day, seven days a week."

"When one is gone, the other is there—there's never a dropped beat," Ralph agrees. "We have seven partners in our practice, so we seldom operate together anymore unless someone requests it. But we still work together on transplants involving living relatives, where I will retrieve the organs and he will put them in."

Although Robert and Ralph have always had a strong influence on each other's lives, they initially had different ambitions. Robert had originally dreamed of becoming a musician like their late father, Rafael Mendez, the world-renowned concert trumpet player and recording artist whose talent earned him a star on Hollywood Boulevard. Ralph, on the other hand, was drawn to medicine from the very beginning.

"Though Robert and I had toured for years, playing the trumpet in concerts with our dad in the Hollywood Bowl and the largest arenas in Europe, it was nothing like watching an operation," recalls Ralph. I went to Stanford pre-med and haven't stopped since."

Robert didn't share his brother's initial enthusiasm for medicine.

"At the particular operation that Ralph found so exhilarating, I fainted," he recalls. But, encouraged by Ralph, Robert finally decided to pursue medicine himself—and it was he who encouraged Ralph into the specialty they now share. Ralph and Robert remain close. Whether silently performing intricate surgical procedures together or playing a trumpet duet, one thing is for certain—Ralph and Robert's unspoken connection has clearly enhanced their successes.

Ralph (left) and Robert Mendez take a break after performing kidney surgery, St. Vincent's Medical Center, Los Angeles.

Tia Mowry
Tamera Mowry

*"T*ia, there's a problem," her boyfriend says.
"What problem?" asks Tia.
"Your sister."
"What about her?"
"When we hang out together, she's kind of, you know, in the way!"
"Really?"

Tia laughs as she recalls the script of this *Sister Sister* sitcom episode. It's said that art imitates life, and, in fact, most of the show's episodes are based on the lives of these nineteen-year-old twin sisters, Tia and Tamera Mowry.

"The producers and writers of the show wanted it to be as real as possible," explains Tamera, "so that twins can relate to the show." The series, now in its fifth season, was developed around the Mowrys. "Basically, we have the say-so because we're twins!"

"And a lot of people don't know what goes on inside of twins," Tia adds. "I don't think anybody

can understand completely unless they are a twin—or the parent of one."

On the show, Tia and Tamera star as seventeen-year-old identical twins who were separated at birth and raised apart until Tamera's conservative father and Tia's outspoken mother decided to live together to reunite their daughters.

"On the show, I'm the smart one, the studious, sensitive, and conservative one," Tia explains. "And Tamera's the mischievous, vibrant, outgoing one." Ironically, in real life Tia and Tamera's personalities are the opposite of their television personas.

"I just watch her and she studies me," laughs Tamera, explaining how they learn to portray their sitcom personalities. She and her sister exchange glances, turning their heads like two synchronized hand puppets.

Tia and Tamera's twinship landed them a spot in a classic commercial. "We've been in the

Tia (left) and Tamera Mowry take a break from filming on the Warner Brothers Studio lot in Burbank, California.

Wrigley's Doublemint gum commercial with other twins!" exclaims Tia.

Tia and Tamera pride themselves on their differences—which are more than just the distinguishing mole on Tamera's left cheek.

"We balance each other out," explains Tia.

"When Tia sees a person out on the street, she'll be the first one to say, 'Hey, what's up?' I have to check them out first. I stay in the corner and if Tia's fine with them, then okay, I go along. But I'm always the one cracking jokes. I don't do it on purpose."

"She'll be giving a serious speech," Tia interrupts, "then she'll make a face, and the whole class is laughing. She's so animated with her face.

"The biggest challenge of being twins is having people see you as individuals," continues Tia. "A lot of times we wouldn't get jobs because we were twins. They didn't want to upset the one who wasn't chosen. One time, the producers liked both of us but they had only one position. So they put both our pictures face down and just chose one. We never felt that we got a job because of our own talents. Other times they would tell our agent, 'Just send one of them out for the audition.' That would really hurt our feelings because we are two different people. We don't have one brain. We just look alike, that's all. And that's the hardest thing to establish. It's still a problem today."

"We see ourselves as a team, like Lucy and Ethel," says Tamera. "We were never jealous of one another. But when people say, 'Hey twins,' they are labeling us as one person instead of calling us by our names. You don't say, 'Hey, boy, come here!'"

The Mowry sisters admit that dating as a twin can be more difficult. "Guys don't know which one to choose, and that's a problem," says Tamera. "We always ask them, 'Why were you attracted to me?'"

Tia jumps in, "When guys can't tell us apart or say, 'I'll take both of you,' I say, 'Excuse me, I don't think so! We're different people!' Or, if I go out with somebody and we break up and he tries to ask Tamera out, that's a big no-no." Luckily, they have different tastes. "If a guy's not funny or can't dance, I say, 'See ya,'" laughs Tia.

"He's got to be tall," smiles Tamera.

Although these Pepperdine University freshmen bicker like most siblings, they love being twins.

"It's funny—when people look at twins they think something's weird or different because we have this bond. People ask, 'Are you guys for real, or is this fake?' I want people to know that the love we have for each other is real," Tia says.

"It's a bond," explains Tamera. "It's a gift from God."

"We're so much closer than regular siblings," Tia says.

"I think it's because we go through life's trials and tribulations together at the same time," Tamera clarifies.

"And you know how a lot of people in school wanted to be popular and tried to fit in? Tamera and I were like, 'I have my sister, my built-in best friend.' In high school, we were so close that we had friends, but not best friends. Now, we have one best friend that we share."

They are extremely close, sharing a car, job, and most college classes—and they admit that they are avoiding separation.

"Tia and I will deal with it when it happens. I don't know what I'll do, so I don't even want to think about it." Tamera pauses. "Maybe we'll work together, so that way we'll see each other every day."

"The longest time we've been separated was about six hours," says Tia. "When I'm by myself I feel like something's missing. It's like I have to feel her, like, 'Okay, she's here.' Even when I had a boyfriend, when I was out with him, I felt incomplete. He just didn't add up to my sister."

They devised a system on dates. "She would page me," explains Tamera, "and say, 'How are you doing?' so I could feel that closeness. My boyfriend really didn't understand it."

runs to their mom, but we ran to each other's room instead."

"I wanted to see if she was okay. But it was funny because we collided—boom!"

"She knocked me down," laughs Tia.

"Then we went to our mom's room," Tia and Tamera say in unison.

"We talk a lot," Tamera admits. "Our publicist and our mother tell us, 'Don't talk at the same time.' We just can't help it. It's literally impossible. It's a twin thing!"

Tia and Tamera have grown up in a close family that encourages honesty, communication, and love. They have two younger brothers, four-year-old Tavior and eleven-year-old Tahj, who both love sports and hope to work in the entertainment business. In fact, Tahj, who made appearances on

"The longest time we've been separated was about six hours. When I'm by myself I feel like something's missing."

"I was jealous of him and he was jealous of me," admits Tia. "I don't know how we're going to do it when we get married. Someone said that we have to get boyfriends at the same time."

Tia and Tamera smile as they recall some unique twin experiences.

"One time we were in a store and I thought I was looking in a mirror, but it was my sister!" exclaims Tia.

"The freakiest thing that Tia and I have noticed about being twins," says Tamera, "is that we have the same nightmares. It's happened all our lives."

"And we were surprised when we had an earthquake," Tia recalls. "Usually everyone

Full House and now has his own sitcom, *Smart Guy*, first introduced his sisters to show biz. Their father, Timothy, is a retired first sergeant in the U.S. Army, and their mother, Darlene, retired as a military drill sergeant to become her daughters' manager in the entertainment business.

Tia and Tamera are proud of their family's closeness and unity.

"We say family time is our quality fun time. Every Sunday is family day," relates Tamera.

Boris Fisch
Joseph Fisch

Seventy-five-year-old identical twins Boris and Joseph Fisch feel blessed to be alive today to tell their story. Millions of others—including their parents and one sister—perished in the Holocaust during World War II. The brothers' love for one another, their teamwork, and their faith in God helped them survive.

In a thick Hungarian accent, Boris tells the story of how he and his twin survived Nazi labor and concentration camps. "At eighteen, before we were taken to concentration camps, we were placed in a forced labor camp in Hungary because Jewish people weren't drafted into the Hungarian army anymore. We built airports, roads, and foundations for buildings."

"For three years, we moved from one place to another, with hardly anything to eat and no pay, going wherever the Hungarian army needed workers," Joseph adds. "We slept where the horses stay, in stalls. But Boris and I were always

together. They tried to separate us, but we always managed somehow."

"We didn't dress alike anymore—"

"—so they wouldn't notice that we looked alike," Joseph finishes.

The brothers endured freezing temperatures and near-starvation on their long, grueling marches from one site to the next.

"After the Germans occupied Hungary in 1943," Boris remembers, "a couple hundred of us Jewish boys had to march to work on the Austrian-Hungarian border. Joseph and I stayed behind with some other boys, hiding in little towns for a couple of weeks. If we were found, we would have been executed.

"We met some Jewish people from Budapest," he continues. "We hitched rides toward Budapest, which was just starting to be occupied by Germany. We had to wear yellow armbands on our left arms or yellow Jewish stars on our chests near our hearts to show that we were

Joseph (left) and Boris Fisch sit at the synagogue where Boris is a cantor in Hallandale, Florida.

Jewish. If we hid our identity, they would kill us. Little by little, the German army started to spread across Europe. Jewish ghettos started to organize in Budapest. All the Jewish people had to leave their homes and gather in big buildings. It was very dangerous for a Jewish person to walk on the streets, because the Germans organized the Hungarian army and anti-Semitic civilians against the Jews. To give an example, if they found a big building that housed Jewish people, the Hungarian army lined the residents up—hundreds of them—on the beach of the Danube River and shot them dead. They fell right into the river."

"We were hiding in a basement in one of those ghettos for almost a week," Joseph says. "Hundreds and hundreds of people died in the ghettos from starvation."

"Some Hungarian civilians provided us with food, but not much," Boris adds. "They called us 'ninety-pound weaklings.' Then the Hungarian military started putting Jewish people in cattle cars headed for Germany. We heard news that the Jewish people from other countries—Poland, Romania, other parts—were taken to terrible concentration camps like Auschwitz."

The brothers were told to pack whatever belongings they had and report to the railroad station. "There were at least one hundred and twenty of us crowded into the cattle cars, but room for only forty," Joseph recalls. "But through a little window, we were able to ask railroad workers for bread in exchange for some women's clothing and shoes we had found while hiding. A worker secretly brought us a big round loaf of Hungarian bread. Everybody in the car was starving and said it wasn't fair that only we had bread. So we gave everybody a little piece. What could we do?"

Fortunately for the Fisches, the German army needed workers in the Bruck An Der Leitha concentration camp in Austria. Once they arrived, German officers collected all the valuables—cigarettes, tobacco, gold, silver, watches, and chains—into a big tablecloth. "They took everything away from us," Joseph says. "Then they divided us up to dig trenches on the Austria-Hungary border so that their enemies, like the Russians, couldn't take over Hungary. It was freezing around December. There was no heat, nothing."

"Sometimes we got caught in rain or snowstorms," Boris adds.

"They gave us coffee, which was really just colored water," recalls Joseph, "and a loaf of bread for twenty people to share."

"We saw many of our friends die."

"We thought we were next—who knows? We weren't afraid anymore," says Joseph. "The rich kids died like flies, but the poor people like us lived. Some people didn't want to suffer anymore, so they said they didn't want to work, and the Germans shot them."

"They figured they were going to die anyway," Boris whispers.

"All of a sudden, an SS man—a sadist who beat people to death every day—began favoring us."

"We thought he took a liking to us because we were good workers."

"He would take us to the kitchen for food," Joseph explains. "We couldn't figure out why. At the time we didn't know it, but we later heard that they were feeding us to send to the German doctor, Josef Mengele, who performed awful experiments on identical twins. Twins were guinea pigs, and almost all of them died. But, luckily, he couldn't send us to Mengele because the American and Russian soldiers started to come, around March 1944."

But in springtime the Fisches found themselves forced on another journey. "We were told to pack up and march twenty miles without food to the shore of the Danube. There, we boarded crowded freight boats heading to Mauthausen, a very terrible concentration camp in Austria," Boris remembers.

"We were on the boat for nine days and nine nights, with no food. But, luckily, Boris and I hid in a chicken coop on deck. All the rest of the people had to go down below," says Joseph. "Out of seven hundred Jewish people on board, only about one hundred and fifty survived. Everybody else died of hunger."

Again, the Fisches' dedication to each other saved their lives. Joseph explains: "Before the trip, we had been ordered to clean up a railroad station which was bombed. There, we found cattle cars full of food and tobacco, so we took some with us on board. We were lucky because we helped each other. If I found some tobacco, and my brother found some marmalade, we'd share."

"We were determined to survive," Boris states. "We told each other, 'We will go back home, we will not die here, and we will fight for our lives.'"

"So you know what we did?" Joseph asks. "Ten of us who believed in God got together and started to pray and cry out to God. And all ten of us are alive today. God listened to our prayers."

"Our parents were watching us from heaven, so that nothing should happen to us," Boris acknowledges. "There's no such thing that you are alone. God is always with you. And some people didn't believe this. Every day, when people died and the SS men threw them overboard, my brother and I said a memorial prayer for that person. We're cantors with a very good Jewish education. The SS officers found out about our prayers and called for us. We thought they were going to kill us." Instead, the brothers were asked to sing prayers for the dead.

"Maybe they believed in their God," says Boris. "And they didn't want God to punish them." "Who knows?"

The Fisches survived the trip, but their hardships were just beginning. "To get off the boat, we had to walk on a narrow piece of wood," relates Joseph. "Many people were dizzy from hunger and couldn't walk straight. If they fell into the water, the Germans shot them to make sure they were dead. I was holding Boris because he couldn't walk well, but he said, 'Let go, because I might accidentally throw you in the water.'"

The boat transported them to Mauthausen, which, like Auschwitz, had a gas chamber and a crematorium. Again, the brothers' resourcefulness allowed them to survive.

"We had hidden tobacco in a dirty, old quilt. But when we arrived, they took everything away. I told Joe, 'Maybe they threw it out in

the garbage.' So we got up in the morning and went through all the garbage piles."

"We found it!" Joseph exclaims, still astonished by the odds of such a miracle.

"Can you imagine that? Amazing. Our parents were watching over us," Boris sighs. "And so every day we sold the cigarettes for bread and soup. A cigarette was worth gold. That's how we survived for a long time. We volunteered for everything. They would give volunteers a little extra bread."

People were dying so rapidly that the Germans stacked the bodies in covered pits. Joseph explains, "We took the dead to the big mass graves and said prayers over them."

"One day," begins Boris, "an SS man called us to the barracks and said, 'Please sit down.' We were scared to death. He said, 'Listen, boys, I'm not here to kill you. You can refuse our request, but if you agree you will get food every day.' He handed out six pliers. Guess for what?"

"To take out the gold teeth from the dead people."

"They melted them into golden bars. I looked at my brother, and my brother looked at me. We made up our minds. We will say no. If they want to kill us, let them kill us. We said no and walked out," Boris recalls with tears in his eyes.

The Russians and Americans were closing in on Austria. "One morning, we were told to march forty miles to a small concentration camp built in the middle of a forest," Joseph recalls.

"In our group of three hundred," says Boris, "maybe one hundred survived. Every day people were getting typhus and falling like flies."

"One day we were in the forest and found a dead horse. We were just like lions or tigers after a kill," shudders Boris. "We cut the dead horse into pieces and ate the meat."

"We survived on that horse for two weeks longer."

"But the Germans knew that the Americans and Russians were nearby and time was getting short. One afternoon, we saw American soldiers parachuting down from airplanes over the camp. They didn't know what they were coming into, and the Germans shot all of them," Boris recalls. "None of them made it alive."

The Fisch brothers were finally liberated on May 4, 1945, five days before their twenty-fourth birthday.

"One day, SS officers started offering us food in exchange for our civilian clothing. They wanted to disguise themselves to escape. At three o'clock the next morning, while we were sleeping, somebody came into the barracks. He told us that all the Germans had run away because the enemy was coming, and nobody was watching us. We couldn't believe it. We went with him to the German barracks—and they were gone," Boris says.

"They had left their cigarettes, and even some rifles."

"We ran back to the barracks with a rifle and started to scream, 'We are free! You don't believe it? We have the rifles here!'" Boris remembers. "Everybody was screaming. Those of us who were healthy, about twenty-five of us, started to march to the next town, Wels, which was five miles away. We kissed the American tanks when we saw them, and knocked on the door of the first big building. Three American soldiers, their rifles pointing at us, answered the door.

"We told them, 'We are Jewish people,' and they said, 'Please come in,' all twenty-five of us.

They had heard about the concentration camps. They asked, 'Are you hungry?' Hungry!?" Boris exclaims. "They said, 'Go down to the basement where there is food.' They had boxes and cartons of food—eggs and bread and salami. We drank champagne. 'Eat whatever you want,' they told us. That was a mistake because we got sick. Some people died because their stomachs weren't used to eating."

The American soldiers rescued people from the concentration camp and took them to the hospital. "They sent us to a German farm nearby and said, 'Tell them that the American soldiers sent you to get horses and wagons to go home.'"

"They didn't want to give us a horse and wagon," Joseph says, "but they were scared of the Americans, so they said, 'Take it, take it.'"

"We loaded up the horse and wagon with sacks of potatoes and flour, and rested at the next farmland."

But once there, the Fisch brothers, along with a few other men, got sick. "The typhus hit us. About three days later, we couldn't move anymore," Joseph remembers.

"The farmer took us to the hospital in Wels. I got so sick," Boris says. "I was in a coma for a week or two."

"He was screaming from pain," his twin remembers. "I couldn't listen to it, so I went to a different room."

Boris survived, and the two brothers headed back to Hungary to reclaim their home in a town about two hundred miles from Budapest. "Somebody was living there already, but we chased them out," says Boris. "We didn't know whether our four sisters were alive. At four o'clock one morning, we were frightened by somebody knocking on our window. It was our neighbor, who told us, 'Boys, I have good news for you.' Three of our sisters were alive, after being rescued from the Bergen-Belsen concentration camp. They sent a Red Cross telegram from Sweden to find out if we were alive. When we sent a telegram back, they started to send us packages with clothes and money from Sweden."

Their sisters had learned the trade of dressmaking to earn a living.

"One of our sisters survived because she made beautiful dresses and shirts for the SS men," says Boris.

"We visit them every two or three years," Joseph adds, "and we visit our mother's grave in Hungary together every year. Now our sisters, who are eighty and eighty-five, are very sick with Alzheimer's disease. In old age, the suffering from the concentration camps gets to you."

Boris and Joseph stayed in Hungary for a year after the war ended, then relocated to a displaced persons (DP) camp in Germany before coming to the United States in 1949. They came to Pittsburgh, married, and have continued their work as cantors, singing Jewish prayers in temple. They now live sixteen miles from one another in Florida.

"Every person who lived through the Holocaust could write not one book, but three," says Boris. "But no matter how miserable you are, don't give up hope. Because if you give up hope, you lose everything."

"Even in the worst times twins still hold together," says Joseph. "That's why we're still alive today. Boris and I always helped each other. My father told us, 'My boys, my twins, you'll always be together. Help each other. Never separate from each other. That is my wish.'"

Abigail Hensel
Brittany Hensel

Two young faces with sandy-colored hair intertwined playfully peek around the door. Seven-year-olds Abigail and Brittany Hensel swing the door open, each with a welcoming smile.

"Do you want to see my room?" Brittany invites as she and Abigail climb over the banister and up the stairs. They are followed by their five-year-old brother, Koty, and three-year-old sister, Morgan.

Abby and Britty are amazingly coordinated and agile. Watching their synchronicity, one almost forgets that they were born with a unique condition called *dicephalus,* in which twins share an undivided torso, two arms, and two legs. Abby and Britty each have their own heart, stomach, and spinal column. They share three lungs and many organs at or below the waist, including a single large liver, a bladder, intestines, and a reproductive tract. According to the April 1996 *Life* magazine article in which they were featured, there are only four sets of surviving twins in recorded history with dicephalus. Abby and Britty are pen pals with one such set of girls close to their age.

"I've noticed that there is an immediate bond between the girls and other twins," notes their mother, Patty, an emergency room nurse.

Their father, Mike, a carpenter and landscaper, encourages them to assert their individuality. "We tell them that they have to tell people, 'We were born that way, we're twins and we're not one person, we're two people.'"

"We're two people from top to bottom," Abby chimes in.

Abby and Britty proudly perform a headstand, narrowly missing the TV stand as they roll upright. Their actions seem so natural. Each feels sensations and controls the limb and trunk on her own side exclusively. Although Abby and Britty have separate spinal cords, there are probably connections between the two nervous

Abigail (left) and Brittany Hensel play at their home in a small town of three hundred people.

systems that help them coordinate movement. But their parents note that what now appears second-nature—walking, swimming, and riding a bicycle—initially took extra time, patience, and practice.

"They ride a bike really well," says Mike. "One day, when they first started to learn, they were riding between cars, and Abby was talking. I said, 'Abby, pay attention!' And she said, 'I don't have to, Brittany is!'"

They are in tune not only with each other's movements, but also with respecting each

with her left. At play their different personalities shine through. Abby, who tends to be the leader, takes the paintbrush first and draws two large eyes, then Britty paints the ears. With a bigger appetite than her sister, Abby eats more of the roasted pumpkin seeds in front of them, but the nutrients feed both growing bodies.

"Britty enjoys reading and loves animals, while Abby doesn't," notes Patty. "Britty would bring everything home if she could!"

Britty proceeds to list enthusiastically the family's pets: three dogs, three cats, five kittens, two fish, a rabbit, and a horse. "And, we have twin kittens, Brianica and Nicole," Britty announces, proud of the names she and Abby have chosen.

They suddenly jump up with a unanimous decision.

"Let's play baseball!" they shout in unison.

Grabbing their plastic bat-and-ball set and wearing a custom-made jacket, the girls bound outside.

"We have a seamstress who makes their clothes with a special neckline," explains Patty. "She'll make one side all pink for Britty and one side all blue

"We take turns deciding, or Mommy picks," explains Britty. "I did a coin flip today," Abby says, "because I wanted to take a shower and Brittany didn't want to. I won."

other's emotional needs. They have a well-practiced system of making decisions.

"We flip a coin, we take turns deciding, or mommy picks," explains Britty.

"I did a coin flip today," Abby says, "because I wanted to take a shower and Britty didn't want to. I won." They are good at taking turns—on the phone, in conversation, and even when it comes to receiving a flu shot.

"It was Britty's turn this time," their dad recalls, explaining that the girls share the same circulatory system.

Abby and Britty sit at the kitchen table painting a Halloween pumpkin, sipping cups of hot chocolate—Abby with her right hand, Britty

for Abby. Sometimes she makes the pants where they can switch them and rotate the colors."

Mike warms up his pitching arm. "You should see them play in their softball league," he exclaims proudly. "They're pretty good, and they take turns at bat."

When they step up to the plate, Britty prepares to hit. After a few pitches, she hits one high in the direction of their grazing horse. The girls take off around the bases, falling in a fit of giggles at home plate, narrowly avoiding being tagged out by their mom.

"It's my turn now," Abby declares. This time, a grounder to left field leads

to their second home run of the day, celebrated with high fives all around. When Abby stubs her toe in the excitement, she grabs her foot, and Britty automatically begins to hop with her.

Across the field in the distance, one can see Abby and Britty's grandmother's house, which they visit frequently.

"This area's been really good for them," Mike says of the small town of three hundred. "Pretty much everybody knows them, and they're outgoing. If people are looking at them, they go right up and talk to them. They seem to have a little glow about them." Abby and Britty are well-liked at school, where they are enrolled in a second-grade class with two other sets of identical twins.

But their closeness is not without obstacles.

"It's hard to be twins when I want to go one way and she wants to go the other way," Abby admits. They are constantly aware of each other's welfare because it so intimately relates to their own—especially in dire circumstances. Stricken with a serious case of pneumonia a few years ago, Britty was placed in the hospital for eight days.

"She was so sick, her veins just shut down, so Abby had to take the IV," her mom recalls. Aside from that scare, Abby and Britty have been healthy, and are as active and energetic as any pair of seven-year-olds.

"The nice thing about it is we know where they both are," their dad says.

"People laugh when we say that," adds their mom, "but it really is an advantage."

Abby and Britty don't allow obstacles to interfere with their dreams, although sometimes compromises are needed. While Britty once dreamt of being a dentist and Abby a pilot, they both now hope to become doctors, "like Dr. Quinn, Medicine Woman!" exclaims Britty. "And I want to get married and have children someday," she adds. Other conjoined twins have married and had children.

While adolescence will no doubt present new challenges to these girls, their parents have always been optimistic and supportive of their daughters. "It's actually been pretty simple for us," Mike says.

"They've been healthy," adds their mom, explaining that Abby and Britty have needed no extraordinary medical care since the removal of a vestigial arm at four months of age. "People have come up to their doctor and said, 'the poor things,'" Patty continues, "but the doctor responds, 'Their glass isn't half empty—it's half full! They're doing better than many kids who are not born conjoined!'"

Abby and Britty sit down at the piano to play a new song they have learned before heading off to bed.

"It's like a slumber party every night," jokes their mom, winking at her daughters as she tucks them under the covers. "One thing you two like is being awake at night and talking to each other when you're supposed to go to sleep!"

After she kisses each goodnight, Patty says softly, "If they had to be put together, I think they were put together perfectly."

Aldo Andretti
Mario Andretti

Most people recognize Mario Andretti as the world's greatest race car driver. He has won at all levels of competition. He was the first driver to win Indy car races in four different decades and was named "Driver of the Quarter Century" in 1992.

What many people don't know is that fifty-eight-year-old Mario Andretti is an identical twin. His brother, Aldo, shares the same talent and passion for racing.

Mario and Aldo's love of the sport began in Montona, Italy, where they were born in 1940. As Italy struggled to recover from the ravages of the Second World War, the Andretti family moved to a refugee camp in Tuscany, where they lived for seven years. Mario and Aldo remember their first exposure to professional racing—as kids peering through a fence to watch the Italian Grand Prix in Monza, Italy.

"I was hooked," says Mario. "From that day on, motor racing was all that Aldo and I talked about. We'd hide under our blankets at night in the refugee camp and pretend we were race car drivers." The brothers thought that it was the closest they would ever come to their dream.

The Andretti family emigrated to the United States in 1955, when Aldo and Mario were fifteen years old. They settled in Nazareth, Pennsylvania—where, conveniently, there was a race track.

"We built our own car in 1958, pooled our money, and were on the track by 1959, when we were nineteen," Mario says proudly. "Aldo would drive one weekend, I would drive the next."

Unfortunately, Aldo had two terrible accidents that ended his driving career. The first occurred in 1959, at the end of the brothers' first racing season. "He came out of that with a head injury," Mario recalls. "He was in a coma for several days. Our parents didn't even know we were racing because they worried about

Aldo (left) and Mario Andretti reminisce in Nazareth, Pennsylvania, where they first settled in the United States.

safety. So I had to be the one to tell them. That was probably the worst moment of my life, really."

"At first they didn't expect me to live," Aldo says. "When I came out of the coma, my thinking and my reactions were slow. I even had to learn how to walk again."

Aldo did recover completely—and raced for ten more years before a second accident forced him to retire.

"A guy who was the track champion spun down the straightaway and hit him in an open-cockpit car," Mario says. "His face had to be rebuilt. That's why we don't look alike anymore. In fact, his nose is much nicer than mine!"

"Yeah, the doctors took care of that!" Aldo laughs.

Mario's career continued. "I was feeling for Aldo because I knew how

day after Indianapolis pole qualifying, the front row has a picture taken, and it's sold immediately. But I didn't want to sit in it because I was so damn ugly because of my burns, so I asked Aldo to do it. Nobody ever questioned it! Now that the story's out, in some circles that photo has become rare. People pay a lot of money for it!"

But Aldo felt uneasy about it. "I felt kind of stupid, to be honest with you, because qualifying in the front row in the Indianapolis 500 is quite an honor and achievement. I felt like an impersonator, like I didn't deserve to be there, other than doing Mario a favor."

Aldo decided to focus his life in another direction after his 1969 accident. "Back in 1970, I saw a business opportunity that I didn't want to slip by. Mario was kind of pressing for us to

"There was always the wish, 'I'm capable of doing that, I wish it would have been me.' . . . It's a little bittersweet. I loved for him to do well. I just wished it was me!"

much I enjoyed what I was doing. I knew that's where he wanted to be," he recalls, "but I never, ever detected a moment of jealousy or of Aldo feeling sorry for himself. I've always admired that in him because I'm not sure I would have been that strong myself. I honestly feel that whenever I achieved a championship or a milestone in my career, he was there cheering for me first and foremost."

"Racing is just like show business—you need the opportunity and the breaks," Aldo says, "and Mario's had them. He had the ability to make it happen, and he was noticed. He was given some good opportunities which I wasn't able to get. There was always the wish, 'I'm capable of doing that, I wish it would have been me.' But I was happy for him also, you know. It's a little bittersweet. I loved for him to do well. I just wished it was me!"

In a photograph that has become a collector's item, it *was* Aldo. "In 1969, I had an accident. My face was burned pretty badly," Mario recounts. "Then I went to Indianapolis and I qualified in the front row. Tradition has it that the

form a partnership. After we stayed in business for about fifteen years, I decided to go on my own. It was a mutual, amicable separation. We just said, 'Let's be brothers and not be partners!'"

"Aldo became a very prominent business-man," Mario explains. "He turned a negative into a positive for himself. He has had a very meaningful and full life and career up to now, but racing was not meant to be for him, although he still loves the sport."

"It's been a lot of effort," says Aldo of his successful machine shop in Indianapolis, which supplies very specialized parts to automotive manufacturers and hospitals. "Personally, I never lucked into anything; I worked hard for everything I got. It's just what my dad always said, 'You reap what you sow.' That was always my character, my focus—'Reach for the stars and settle for a ladder to get there.'"

Their home lives began to differ at an early age. "I got married when I was twenty-one years old. My life took a different path," Aldo continues. "I concentrated on doing things locally in Nazareth. Mario, still single, was able to do more traveling and expand his racing career. I moved to the Midwest in 1964, for a better future for my family."

"But, our relationship has always been good, excellent. We were never really apart all our lives, in a sense," says Mario. "There was never a time when we didn't speak to one another for any reason. We shared everything. My mother was always dressing us the same, which I hated, until we came to this country at age fifteen."

"I hated that!" Aldo agrees. "I never wanted to wear his clothes. As a matter of fact, even when the clothes were clean, I wanted to make sure what I was wearing was mine, so we used to smell for it. We'd smell and say, 'Well, that's mine.' My mom was meticulous about cleanliness and used to get so mad."

"The only hardship of being a twin," declares Mario, "was that we had to share everything. It didn't hurt me psychologically. It was just, 'Gee, my buddy has a bicycle and I have half a bicycle. I don't know whether I own the front end or the back end.' I never sent Aldo a birthday card, and he never sent me one! We joke about that one. I say, 'I know when your birthday is—but I'll be damned if I'm going to send you a card!'"

Yet their competitiveness was just as strong as their closeness.

"When we were on the track at the same time," Mario admits, "you're darn right we were competitive. To me, he was just another faceless competitor. I wanted to beat him as much as he wanted to beat me. But that's natural. It's a good type of competition, not a negative competition. We each had a goal to do the best for ourselves. It was not a matter of, 'Oh, gee, let him win—I want him to smile,' you know. None of that."

. . .

"There are advantages and disadvantages to being twins," Aldo states. "Growing up, you hear the same things—'Oh my God, look at them, they are just like two drops of water. They are so identical, they even sound alike.' That got kind of old. And when Mario was quite famous, I would go to dinner or sit at a lunch counter, and people would start staring and looking around like I had two heads. Sometimes it's gratifying and sometimes it's annoying. But, occasionally, if it's a tense situation, it's an advantage—it's a conversation piece."

"When people ask us, 'What's it like to be a twin?'" says Mario, "we respond, 'Well, what's it like not to be a twin?' You can't describe it. I don't know any other way of life. I don't think there's anything more extraordinary about twins, to be honest with you. It's just different, it's a miracle of life, it's what God gave us."

Claudia Jefferson Beckman
Colleen Jefferson Hisdahl

Colleen Jefferson Hisdahl was driving home on a dark night when she suddenly collided with the back of a big semi-truck with no break lights. Miles away, her identical twin sister, Claudia, knew Colleen was in trouble.

"I can't even describe how I felt. It was the weirdest thing. Something was wrong, something wasn't right," says thirty-five-year-old Claudia Jefferson Beckman as she describes the unusual connection between Colleen and herself.

"All of a sudden I felt an uneasiness," Claudia continues, "so I called home and told my mom, 'Colleen's been in a car accident.' Right after I hung up, the police called my parents and told them what had happened. Colleen was shaken up but was all right."

Colleen and Claudia accept these experiences without demanding an explanation. Both speak with a sincere enthusiasm to "tell it like it happened" rather than to convince anyone of the truth of their stories. And they have many stories—starting with early childhood.

"We had our own language until we were almost four," Claudia says with a laugh. "All I know is we called each other 'Ca.' My brother could understand a lot of it, for some reason. My parents were a little concerned that we wouldn't be able to start kindergarten!"

Although Colleen and Claudia do not recall their twin language, remnants of their communication surface from time to time.

As Claudia recalls, "Not too long ago, I was home visiting my parents, when my mom woke up in the middle of the night. She heard Colleen and me talking in our sleep to each other, in our baby twin talk."

Colleen relates another amazing incident, this one more recent. "We both have jaw problems. I had surgery to fix mine because it was worse than Claudia's. After numerous surgeries, I had some facial paralysis on one side."

Colleen Jefferson Hisdahl (left) and Claudia Jefferson Beckman walk Colleen's dog, Mandy, on Bald Eagle Lake, near Minneapolis.

"After one of Colleen's jaw surgeries, I developed Bell's palsy—temporary facial paralysis on one side," Claudia describes. "It turns out that the paralysis was on the same side as Colleen's nerve damage. At the time, we didn't know that Colleen's face was paralyzed from the surgery, because her face was still wrapped up."

The sisters are often asked about their shared sixth sense.

"People would doubt us at first," says Colleen, "but now they don't because they see it happen so often." One such person is their mother.

"Claudia was at college in another state," Colleen explains, "and I was at home with my parents. In the middle of the night, I suddenly developed intense chest pain. My parents always unplug their phone at night, so I ran into their room, 'Plug in the phone, plug in the phone—something happened to Claudia!' Mom plugged in the phone and it was ringing. It was the emergency room calling. Claudia had had a really bad choking experience—she had choked on a peanut M&M and the doctors thought it was lodged in her lungs."

Claudia, barely able to wait for her sister to finish, describes another story, "Colleen fell in a hole while playing Frisbee, and our mom rushed her to the hospital." Claudia was not there and knew nothing about the accident at the time.

"I called my friend Greg and said, 'Colleen got hurt. We have to go to the hospital.' I don't know how I knew. Nothing hurt. I just knew something was wrong. Greg drove me to Mounds Park Hospital, where Colleen always went if she was injured. When we got there, my mom just about dropped. She shook her head and said, 'They just put her in one of the cubicles in the emergency room.'"

Although their twinship seems to come naturally to them, Colleen and Claudia have a bond forged by years of hard work. They describe difficult times of being compared, of intense competition, and of the struggle they endured to developed their own identities.

Colleen half jokes, "Growing up, we didn't get along unless we were getting into trouble. If Claudia took a right turn, I took a left. I wanted to be everything she wasn't because we were always compared."

They blame a lot of their early fights on identity struggles and reactions to the way people compared them.

"I think the hardest thing about being a twin," says Colleen, "is when people immediately look at you and want to see differences. They don't want to get to know you as a person. I think competition causes some twins to hate each other.

"The teachers would say, 'Your sister is good at that, why aren't you?'" recalls Colleen.

Luckily, these sisters grew up in a close-knit family with two older brothers, an older sister, and very supportive parents who raised them as two separate people. "When I run into anyone who has twins," says Claudia, "the first thing I tell them is, 'Let them be who they are. Let them know their first names.' In school, we didn't know we had first names—we were called 'the twins.' Our parents would say, 'They're not *the twins,* they're Claudia and Colleen.'"

There were times, however, when Claudia and Colleen played down their differences.

"Once Colleen had a blind date and didn't feel like going," Claudia admits, "so I went for her. He and Colleen ended up dating for six months. I never told him that I sat in for her first date! The best is, when Colleen would answer the phone and didn't want to talk, she'd pretend to be me and say, 'She's not home right now.'"

Colleen chimes in, "Or when I go to the store and decide to run in real quick even though I look like a mess. If I run into someone I know, I say, 'Oh, hi, I'm Claudia. I'm in town visiting Colleen.'"

Despite their closeness, the sisters live surprisingly independent lives. After attending separate colleges, they now live in different states, Colleen in Minnesota and Claudia in Illinois. And their jobs, although similar in many ways, are far from identical: Colleen is both a fire fighter and a counselor for emotionally disturbed children and adults, while Claudia is a member of the Marine Corps Reserves and a teacher for emotionally and behaviorally disturbed children. Both are married.

Claudia says that "you can't compare the relationship between a spouse and a twin. They are so different. It's not like my husband is second fiddle, it's a different fiddle! He's my best friend, and so is Colleen."

Colleen admits that, because of their closeness, "it's very hard to live apart. We call each other on the telephone three, four, five times a week. We'll sip coffee and talk on the phone while getting ready for work. When we do get together, the hardest part is leaving and knowing I'm not going home with Claudia."

Despite the distance between them, Claudia and Colleen remain closer than ever.

"When I run into anyone who has twins, the first thing I tell them is, 'Let them be who they are. Let them know their first names.'"

Marion Bartholomew
Minerva Lipp

"How does my outfit look, Minerva?" Marion asks as she models her off-white, linen three-piece suit for her twin sister. The ninety-three-year-old identical twins are preparing for the evening's reunion.

This isn't just any reunion, either. It happens to be Minerva Lipp's and Marion Bartholomew's seventy-fifth high school reunion at Bay Shore High School. The two sisters stick together now just as they did growing up.

"We were the only children in our family," explains Minerva, "and we were perfectly happy just to be together, period."

Nearly a century later, their relationship hasn't changed much; but the same can't be said for the world. Since their birth in 1904, Marion and Minerva have witnessed the transitions from horse-and-buggies to automobiles, from the Wright Brothers' first flight to NASA space shuttle missions, and from doctor's house calls to managed care.

"Back then, movies were a nickel and so was a loaf of bread," says Marion. "The most amazing invention was the airplane. I remember in the old days when an airplane went over the house. We ran outside, stood in the middle of the road, and looked up at it in awe. We remember the day Lindbergh left from an airfield on Long Island, on the first solo transatlantic flight. He took off only a few miles from our house—on the north shore of Long Island, while we were on the south shore. We listened to the radio all night about his progress and prayed that he would make it!

"And my dad had one of the first cars that came out; it was called the Franklin," continues Marion, "a low, sporty type. And boy, that was a big thing! Every Sunday afternoon, we'd take a ride around the island."

In those days, there were no televisions and few sports for women, but the sisters had no

Marion Bartholomew (left) and Minerva Lipp spend winters in Florida, at Marion's house.

trouble entertaining themselves. "We were tomboys," says Minerva. "Our father was a builder. We loved visiting the lumberyard, climbing tall buildings and jumping from roof to roof. In the back of the lumberyard, there was a 150-foot-high iron water tower, and we'd climb an iron ladder that was bolted to it all the way to the top. On our way up the tower, we'd swing back and forth from the inside to the outside of

me, 'What's he like?' I said, 'Oh, he's very nice. Why don't you go out with him sometime and find out for yourself?' So for the next date, I stayed in the kitchen when he arrived at 8:00 P.M. He picked up Minerva and they went to the movies and the ice cream store. He never found out that we switched places!"

But on the "date" Minerva nearly gave the secret away. "The two were chatting away when Minerva said, 'Marion and I, so and so,' and he looked at her and said, 'Marion?' And she recovered by saying, 'Oh, my best friend's named Marion, too.'"

Their ability to fool people started from the beginning, as Minerva recounts—the very beginning. "In those days, women gave birth at home, and our mom didn't expect twins. When she went into labor, the nurse called the doctor, who came in a horse-and-buggy. It took a little time for him to get there. In the meantime, the nurse had to deliver me—what they

"Nowadays, things are different, and twins are all over the place. You have to have quadruplets to get any attention today!"

the ladder until we reached the top, where we could see for miles around us. I would die if I saw my child do that!

"Besides being great swimmers, we were never into other sports. We'd rather climb water towers or old buildings. And we'd walk to school in those days. We'd look out the front door first to make sure nobody was coming along that we had to walk with because we just wanted to be by ourselves. We had that togetherness. All through the years we've been very close. We took piano lessons while we were growing up and often played duets together on two pianos at recitals."

They also played some tricks on other people together.

"I was dating a young man from the next village," Marion recollects, "and Minerva asked

thought was *the* baby. But when the doctor arrived, he checked and said, 'Oh, there's another one!'"

"So then I came along and there were two of us," Marion laughs.

"Because twins were less common back then, we received a lot of attention when our mom walked down the street with us. In those days, most twins dressed alike—it was the style. Nowadays, things are different, and twins are all over the place. You have to have quadruplets to get any attention today!" jokes Minerva.

Both sisters were married soon after graduating from Bay Shore High School, and each for almost fifty years. "I was married first," recalls Minerva. "Marion said, 'I don't think I'll ever find somebody as nice as your George.' But two years later she found Billy, and she and Billy got married Billy worked for the William Liddell Linen Business, and my husband,

George, worked for the L. E. Waterman Fountain Pen Company."

Marion's father-in-law worked for the company that supplied food for the *Titanic*. "My father-in-law was a good friend of Captain Edward John Smith and was set to sail on the *Titanic*'s maiden voyage. But he was suddenly stricken with a serious illness. He and his baggage were taken off the ship. I would never have met my husband had his father gone on the ship. It was his father who later encouraged Billy to travel from Liverpool, England, to America, where I met him.

"Strangely enough," Marion continues, "our husbands passed away unexpectedly only two months apart," explains Marion. "It was soon after my husband and I relocated to Florida that George passed away in May, and Billy in July. As soon as my husband died, I took the next plane home to be with Minerva. And three months later, Minerva suggested, 'It would be a great idea if we lived in your house in Florida in the winter and you lived here in Long Island with me in the summer, away from the heat!' So we both cried and hugged each other   and we've been sharing our homes ever since, for the past twenty-two years. We get along beautifully. We have such a wonderful understanding. We're of one mind."

Minerva and Marion, nicknamed "the M&M twins" by their friends, spend summers in Bay Shore, New York, the town where they grew up.

"We love each other dearly," adds Minerva. "Everybody says we don't know how lucky we are—but we do!"

The sisters have remained very active—going to the beach, playing bridge, taking afternoon drives, and visiting friends. "I'm sorry not everyone has a twin sister or brother," says Marion. Judging by what the two have shared, it's easy to see why.

"You know, we went through very rough times," Minerva relates. "We went through three wars and the Depression. But we've always kept our chins up—and we've always made it. It's no wonder we go on being healthy, happy, and free. We've had such blessings all along the way—a wonderful family and good health." Neither of them has ever been admitted to a hospital, except for giving birth.

"I have two loving, adorable daughters, Virginia and Carole," Marion explains. "And, between Minerva and me, we have eight great-grandchildren." Minerva raves about her son, George, who was born with a twin brother who died shortly after birth. "He's wonderful—even superer than super," she brags.

"When George was about two years old, Marion spent six weeks in England. On her return, when Marion and I walked in the front door together, George stared at the two of us, toddled over to me and, looking up, said, 'Mommy!' Then he turned to his Aunt Marion and said, 'More Mommy!'"

Minerva and Marion smile as they sit on matching chaises on their back porch. They peer up at the beautiful, cloudless, summer sky, enjoying life and wondering what more lies ahead.